Every. Night. Of.
The. Week.

This book is for my family.
Those I have created beautiful chaos with, then hugged
with all my heart – Andrew, James, Beau & Winter.
Those I have laughed with till I peed – Charlotte, Alex & Toby.
Those who ferociously guided me through life and
who I miss so much every day – Mum & Dad.
You are my favourite collection.

Every. Night. Of. The. Week.

Sanity solutions for the daily dinner grind

Lucy Tweed

murdoch books

Sydney | London

Contents

Monday 15

Lifting the negative curse with a fresh and pretty facelift on a week day that should make us bounce.

Tuesday 41

The week can be judged today. You know by now whether you are set for a long haul or a sweet little wander.

Wednesday 67

Looking forward is good on hump day, but looking back you'll notice that's where ALL the missing socks are.

One-sided icebreaker

Everything I love, I love with saturating intensity. Food is not the exception; it's the first passionate relationship I had.

When I was 4 I would relish eating warm buttery toast in bed at a way-too-early hour (thanks Dad for indulging me). Then I'd climb into my parents' bed and complain about pointy scraps in the sheets, earning me the title of Princess Fancy Crumb.

At age 7 or so I had a play date who brought a tin of wonderfully artificial home-brand spaghetti. Lunch that day would be the stuff of dreams. No fig, ham and cheddar grazing plates, no garden herb omelette made from our own hens' eggs, no Promite and sprouts on dark caraway rye – that day, we would dine on something loaded with sugar and salt, yet completely bland and utterly without flair or emotion. My excitement was palpable.

The heartbreak set in the moment Mum delivered our plates to the table. She had lightly heated the food (unnecessary but acceptable) and then stirred through an equal quantity of roughly torn flat-leaf parsley that was so robust it had surely twice seeded.

Fury and tears inevitably followed. Looking back, I'm convinced the PTSD from this incident motivated me to become the curator of everything that goes into my mouth.

By the time I was 9 I knew how to separate eggs to make mayonnaise and meringues, but also the perfect quantity of water + time on the stove + seasoning to get the most Shirley Temple tasty bounce out of a 2-minute noodle.

Then there was the boscaiola period of 1995 (I still don't understand how something can be SO delicious and sickening at the same time).

As a teen, I had an unruly crew of friends who would seek munchie satisfaction in our Bondi kitchen when we'd skip school, eating crushed summer tomato and garlic spaghetti.

And in my first share flat, there was that roast chicken with basil and wine dish by Nigel Slater that changed my life.

Food – all food – became an exciting journey.

If I didn't like something, I wondered why, and tried cooking it in different ways.

For this rather selfish reason I am the cook at home. Not necessarily to nourish my family or to indulge my friends with the gift of feasting; more so to play with the thing I love, to replicate something I have eaten out, to flex a new tool or try a new process.

I am just lucky that my obsession benefits those around me. I've always found it incredibly satisfying to induce appreciative moans in people and so far, making incredible food has been one of the easiest ways for me to do that. Pair that with a weakness for laughter and big gatherings, and the generous facade is complete.

We all win, although I often feel like it's mostly me.

There was a brief interlude when I was a bookkeeper in New York for a now insanely overpriced street-wear label. This pathway of conservatism was soon deemed too black-sheepish for me to maintain, and is now simply a capsule period of fond memories.

I have been a food, lifestyle and event stylist in Sydney for over 20 years, and have recently been able to add food writer and consultant to the bill.

I began this illustrious career under the guidance of Donna Hay. Aside from teaching me to appreciate the beauty of seasonal food, she once said something during a heartbreaking time in my life that has forever made sense: 'You need to prioritise. We are making pretty pictures for a magazine.' I am grateful because this sentiment has allowed me to drive my passion and profession, while keeping love and humour firmly at the top of the list.

This book's namesake is my Instagram account @EveryNightOfTheWeek, which was originally a space for me to document the dinners I made for my family. Mild envy of people with a repetitive repertoire inspired a personalised visual menu board, so I didn't have to think what I was going to make. It also gave me an outlet to love, question and mildly mortify my family (until they began to follow along).

It turns out that the daily struggle and juggle is real, and we are far better off enjoying it all together than alone. Leading neatly to this book.

So while I transcribe the recipes from my mind, you will also get an insight into the energy of each day of the week, along with thoughts and memories. Monday, for instance, is a wonder of potential and good intentions, but by Thursday we are taking stock of the remaining food in the fridge and any burns we've collected along the way. This momentum of the weekly cycle is actually a remedy in itself.

I am very much an instinctual cook, possibly a genetic trait bequeathed to my entire overly creative family. I rely on my lizard brain to penetrate my consciousness at precisely the right second for me to shriek 'F*CK, the chicken!' and retrieve it from the oven, perfectly cooked.

Cooking times are just a guide and so much comes down to common sense. For example, don't walk away when frying or browning. Use your face to judge it – eyes, ears and nose. I taste marinades and sauces as I go, searching my palate for the missing seasoning and adjusting the ratios. I talk to my butcher and fishmonger – a lot. Sometimes even about meat and fish.

I respond to produce that smells and looks fantastic because it's basically the same chemistry as dating; you just know when someone/thing is saying without saying, 'trust me, you want me, I am right for you'.

I do make a few conscious decisions with food and they are primarily to keep it as local and direct as possible and as clean as I can manage. I will turn to a packet shortcut with undisguised desperation, until I notice the ingredients resemble a periodic

table. Understanding the ingredients and replicating the flavour of a favourite store-bought dressing evokes hacker-like satisfaction.

I learn slowly through snippets of information and pleasurable encounters. And while I love inventing a recipe, I know it has found its way to me through centuries of like-minded people, accidentally (or deliberately) discovering new ways to satisfy a craving.

Writing this book has forced me to apply a new level of discipline to my sport. There are measurements, weights and times, the cursing is beeped, and the majority of it was written sitting down.

I encourage you to write amendments all over any recipe you can improve. Everything in this book is subjective. So for those of you who love to cook, you'll know which bits to skim, and if you are new to cooking, welcome!

Essentials

MAKING FRIENDS WITH YOUR COLD AND DRY STORAGE

You have to accept that your pantry is basically an extension of your palate.
Just like your wardrobe … you have to know what suits you, what you are
comfortable with and, of course, what you are missing.

The thing I am still learning in both departments is to throw out all the sh#t
I will never use/wear. I can't tell you how many tins or hangers of 'intentions'
I have in both, but writing this book did some heavy sifting for me.

It comes down to this list really.

FRIDGE

- Eggs
- Milk
- Butter
- Cream
- Greek-style yoghurt
- Cheese (parmesan, mozzarella and haloumi)
- Wine (for drinking, but if you just cook with yours it can be kept in the pantry)

- Fresh herbs
- Fresh ginger
- Mustard (dijon and seeded)
- Capers
- Anchovies
- Mayo
- Sriracha
- White miso paste
- Fish sauce

FREEZER

- Baby peas
- Spinach and/or kale
- Breadcrumbs made from stale bread
- Bacon
- Good sausages
- Mince
- Homemade wontons
- Homemade gnocchi
- Store-bought ravioli
- Pastry (puff and shortcrust)
- Makrut lime leaves
- Bird's eye chillies
- Lemongrass

PANTRY

- Flour (plain/all-purpose and self-raising)
- Dried yeast
- Rice (jasmine and/or basmati)
- Dried pasta (long and short)
- Dry rice noodles
- Sugar (brown and raw)
- Honey
- Oil (olive, extra virgin olive, rice bran and sesame)
- Vinegars (white, white wine, red wine and Chinese black; add balsamic for a 90s vibe)
- Liquid stock (chicken, beef and veg; keep in the fridge if homemade!)
- Chicken stock powder
- Curry paste
- Tinned tuna in olive oil
- Passata
- Tinned tomatoes
- Tinned coconut cream

- Tinned beans, lentils and chickpeas
- Fried shallots
- Shaved coconut
- Panko breadcrumbs
- Soy sauce
- Oyster sauce
- An Asian chilli condiment
- Tamarind paste
- Potatoes (in a cloth bag to keep out the light)
- Garlic
- Onions (brown and red)
- Always lemons and limes

DRIED HERBS AND SPICES

- Peppercorns
- Sea salt
- Oregano
- Rosemary
- Chilli flakes
- Cumin seeds
- Coriander seeds
- Turmeric
- Cinnamon
- Garlic powder
- Onion powder
- Paprika (smoked and sweet)
- Bay leaves
- Cardamom pods

Kit list

I have an even tighter crew when I Airbnb but this
motley selection are the things I reach for daily.

It's enough to keep you confident without getting confused.

HEAVY METAL

- Good non-stick frying pan: try and get one that neatly fits the lid of your biggest saucepan

- Big and little saucepans with lids: essential for boiling, poaching, steaming and souping

- Shallow cast-iron pan, kind of like a frying pan but with two handles, OR a shallow cast-iron baking dish: ideal for lasagne, rice bakes, deep pizzas and much more

- Large flameproof casserole dish or Dutch oven for slow-cooking soups and meats, etc

- Lots of trays and tins: deepish heavy ones for roasting, lighter trays for baking, plus lightweight flat pizza trays (which are great because, being round, they don't buckle; also perfect for crisping chips)

POWER

- High-speed blender: used daily for smoothie-making, spice-grinding, emulsifying bearnies (see page 150)
- Small stick blender with a food chopper attachment: perfect for blending soup, and the attachment does a great onion chop
- Hand-held beaters or a stand mixer: the dough hook acts like a third arm, which I love (I've even used it to coat chicken in mayo when prepping buckets of nuggets)

AMMO

- Mandoline: get one, become a ninja
- A fantastic peeler, not a shitty cheap one
- Microplane: WTF did we do before the surgeon took a bone file home to his wife, who grated zest and nutmeg with speed and instantly trademarked this tool?
- Citrus squeezer: Jamie Oliver's hands are either made of asbestos or he only squeezes lemons through his fingers for TV (or when he doesn't have a paper cut)
- Garlic crusher: it's not about avoiding the smell on your fingers, it's about adding it fast
- Noise-cancelling headphones: for full immersion cooking

- Quick flick tools: wooden spoons, high-heat rubber spatulas, big spoons, tongs, a lifter (like a burger flip), a skimmer, some good scissors
- Knives:
  - A chef's knife: go and feel one, wield it unmenacingly before you buy it – it should feel good in your grip and be nicely weighted (also, learn how to sharpen it properly)
  - Utility knives (I love the little plain and serrated ones with plastic handles): get a few – you'll never cut a tomato with more prowess

FRONTLINE ARTILLERY

- Deep platters, which can hold run-off juices, sauces or dressings: perfect for roasts or large salads
- Bowls for sides and condiments
- A sauce jug (this could also be a jar)
- Lots of jars and bottles, saved from store-bought condiments
- Linen napkins, because damn it, if I've made the effort then the sensation should last beyond chewing and swallowing. Treat yo'self.

Dominating

TIPS AND TRICKS OF THE TRADE

I only become the 'sub' in my kitchen once I am eating, and then I am weak at the knees.

These are things I do quite unconsciously, and in fact I had to think hard about
what they are … but they make my movements while cooking smoother.
Tricks and tips of the trade delivered straight to your door.

- Storing your herbs properly can mean the difference between 3 and 8 days of freshness. Rinse and wrap them in paper towel, put them in a zip-lock bag or airtight container and toss them back in the fridge.

- Similarly, trimming and washing lettuce before you pack it away is both a time saver and extender.

- Icing salad herbs is a stylist trick to keep things perky on set, and worth doing at home too. At the start of making a big salad, pick all your herbs and put them in a large bowl of iced water for about 20 minutes. They will drink and spring up.

- When herbs do start to lose their vibrancy, pick the leaves and discard any that have decayed. Blend the rest with olive oil and store in a jar in the fridge, or freeze in ice-cube trays. What you have there is the perfect flavour hit for grilled meats, pastas and soups, or stir through mayo for a great sambo condi.

- Buy a second thing of steamed rice for the freezer when ordering takeaway. That's half a meal done.

- Save your stale bread. Trim off the dry crusts, tear the bread into chunks and freeze. When you need a crispy crouton, just toss with oil and salt and bake until golden.

- Or blend the bread chunks to a fine crumb to use later in pangrattato, as a lasagne topping or for generally coating things.

- When making schnitty or any procedure involving dipping something to coat, use skewers to eliminate sticky breaded E.T. fingers.

- Make double of anything that you can freeze. Ragu, soup, gnocchi.

- Making wontons or dumplings can be laborious, so if you've made more filling than you can deal with, any excess makes a great midweek stir-fry – it's already seasoned and full of great things.

- Marinate and freeze meat straight from the shop, then all you have to do later is thaw it the night before and bake, fry or barbecue when you get home.

- Buy a whole chicken when you are just not sure what the plan is. Honestly, this is the best. You can roast it whole, barbecue it flat, section and bake with rice, steam, shred, turn it into soup, make salads or sambos … It's the epitome of faking till you make it.

- If you are planning on roasting a chicken, do two. Shred the meat and save it.

- Family-style means eating from the pan and is totally acceptable. As is DIY eating with your hands. This is an obvious 'hack'… so look at it as more of a reminder.

- Make enough dressing for a week.

- Use round sticky dots to label the top of your spice jars. I store mine in a big Tupperware container and this saves me from the intensely irritating lift-and-search method.

- Storing dry goods in jars keeps them all fresh, plus it means basics like flour, sugar and rice all get topped up before they run out because you can see them.

Monday

Monday has energy and potential. Like any cycle, we start with a terribly ambitious outlook. You are gonna keep this pony gunning in the right direction, intent on maintaining a healthy, happy attitude to life in general. The herbs are fresh and the fridge is full.

1 bunch rainbow chard,
leaves removed and torn,
stalks chopped into 1 cm
(½ inch) pieces
6 garlic cloves, chopped
1 onion, chopped
2 teaspoons ghee (olive oil is fine)
1 bunch kale, chopped into 4 cm
(1½ inch) pieces
250 g (9 oz) frozen spinach,
thawed, drained
sea salt and freshly ground
black pepper

500 g (1 lb 2 oz) fresh ricotta
2 eggs, lightly beaten (reserve
1 teaspoon for the egg wash)
handful of dill, chopped
handful of flat-leaf parsley
leaves, chopped
handful of mint leaves, chopped
grated zest and juice of 1 lemon
250 g (9 oz) haloumi, grated
1 tablespoon dried oregano
1 rectangular sheet (or
2 squares) good-quality
shortcrust pastry

1 rectangular sheet (or
2 squares) good-quality
puff pastry
1 tablespoon black and white
sesame seeds

OPTIONAL INGREDIENTS
lemon wedges and, while it
defies tradition, this pie coexists
very well with sriracha and
kewpie mayonnaise

THIS IS AN ABSOLUTE BEAUTY.
It occasionally flares up virally
… in a good way … on my Insta
feed, because once you learn it
you'll make it often. You'll adapt
it and make it your own.

It will become a staple.

Preheat the oven to 180°C (350°F).

In a large frying pan over medium
heat, fry the chard stalks, garlic
and onion in the ghee for
10 minutes.

Turn the heat to high, add the
chard and kale leaves and fry for
a further 5 minutes.

Add the spinach and season,
then remove from the heat and
allow to cool.

In a large bowl, combine the
ricotta, beaten egg (except the
teaspoon you've remembered
to keep back), dill, parsley, mint,
lemon zest and juice, haloumi
and dried oregano. Stir in the
chard mixture.

On a large (50 cm x 30 cm/
20 inch x 12 inch) baking tray
lined with baking paper, place
one rectangular sheet of
shortcrust pastry, or overlap
two square sheets and seal
at the centre.

Spoon the ricotta and chard
mixture on top.

Top with the sheet of puff
pastry, crimp the edges to seal
completely and score using long
diagonal slashes.

Whisk together the reserved
egg and 1 tablespoon of water
to make an egg wash. Brush
over the pastry and sprinkle with
sesame seeds.

Bake for 40 minutes until golden
and puffed.

Serves 8

Super Greens Pie

An aggressive level of greens at the start of the week is a good way to dictate how the rest will play out.

6 cups (1.5 litres) chicken stock
2 corn cobs, kernels removed,
  cobs reserved for the stock
2 tablespoons olive oil
1 onion, finely chopped
3 tablespoons butter
3 garlic cloves, finely chopped
1½ cups (330 g) carnaroli rice
hailstorm of grated parmesan
3 tablespoons finely chopped
  chives

OPTIONAL INGREDIENTS
100 g (3½ oz) stracciatella,
and tomato sauce, because
there's always one jerk who
thinks it can be improved
and tbh it's their life they are
destroying so let them have it

MY HUSBAND IS ACCOUNTS PAYABLE at home, and because of my flippant approach to grocery buying, he's also my home shopper. Do something recklessly enough and it's likely that someone will become so irritated they will take on the role.

Considering my day job though, he doesn't take this exercise lightly at all.

I like to smatter the list with new and exciting things he's never heard of, written in 'doctor script scrawl', then be absent from my mobile while he is hunting and gathering with gusto.

Carnaroli is one example and the state he returned in was arousing. He'd not only tracked down the beast, but slaughtered the head of the pack and returned with a prize brand. And with only 12 (infuriating for him) missed calls.

Place the stock in a saucepan over low heat to warm through, adding the reserved cobs for flavour.

Heat the oil in a large high-sided frying pan or large saucepan over medium heat.

Add the onion and corn kernels and saute until softened and just starting to brown, about 10 minutes.

Add 1 tablespoon of butter, the garlic and rice and cook for a further 2 minutes.

Begin adding the warm stock, a ladle at a time, stirring as you go.

Continue until the rice is a soft creamy texture but with a bit of bite in the centre.

Take the pan off the heat, add a final ladle of stock, the remaining butter, the parmesan and most of the chives.

Give it a really firm handshake of a stir to encourage a glossy, silky finish.

I kept a few corn kernels aside from the frying process to top the risotto along with the last of the chives, which feels like a jazzy little trick for guest impress, but high-fiving each serve with a spoonful of stracciatella cheese (the life blood of a burrata) is nothing short of amazing.

Serves 4–6

Corn Risotto

Sounds revolting, but the texture of risotto is most delicious somewhere between stew and gravy with grains.

Freeform Vegetable Lasagne

The beauty of a freeform: you just put it all in a big baking dish however you like.

2 cups (500 ml) beshy
  (see page 204)
1 cup (130 g) grated mozzarella
250 g (9 oz) fresh lasagne sheets
500 g (1 lb 2 oz) fresh ricotta
grated zest of 1 lemon
1 teaspoon garlic powder
1 tablespoon dried oregano
500 g (1 lb 2 oz) tomato passata
  (pureed tomatoes)
500 g (1 lb 2 oz) pumpkin
  (squash), peeled and
  thinly sliced

1 bunch silverbeet
  (Swiss chard), stalks removed
2 tablespoons olive oil
sea salt and freshly ground
  black pepper

OPTIONAL INGREDIENTS
grated parmesan

LOOK, I GET IT, 1 hour is a long cook time for a Monday dinner and BC* I would have agreed, except, like so many during the height of the pandemic, I found myself pining for the stress of 'just another manic Monday'. So, rather than miss it, I just created it.

Plus we all know 'next day' lasagne is arguably better, so you could get ahead and make it yesterday to reheat today.

It makes lots and freezes well!

Preheat the oven to 180°C (350°F).

Warm the bechamel sauce and whisk in the mozzarella.

Blanch the fresh lasagne sheets in boiling water for a minute. Drain and set aside.

I know, I know … you don't HAVE to, but where I hack and cheat in some recipes, I make it up and add more work in others.

Plus, blanching the lasagne sheets means you can boss them around a bit more and it guarantees a more saucy pie.

Combine the ricotta, lemon zest, garlic powder and oregano until smooth.

Assemble however you like; for my version, do this:

Grab your biggest baking dish (or two). Mine is a big flat salad bowl. The mantra 'what goes into the bowl must come out' does NOT apply.

Passata all in (because it's a Monday and I want to start the week well, I used a jar of vodka sauce, as luck would have it).

Pumpkin, silverbeet leaves and lasagne sheets jumble in. I like to put the pumpkin strips in vertically, do little cluster fists of leaves, and torn ribbons of lasagne.

Then fill all the holes with the lemony ricotta like you would when fixing a hole in a wall – generous dollops mushed in.

Pour the warm cheesy bechamel over the top and drizzle with oil.

Season and bake for 1 hour.

*Before Covid

Serves 8

1 red onion, finely chopped
1 cup (135 g) grated zucchini
  (courgette)
3 tablespoons olive oil
6 garlic cloves, finely chopped
baby fist of chopped
  flat-leaf parsley
½ cup (80 g) frozen kale
½ teaspoon sea salt
50 g (1¾ oz) butter
1 cup (220 g) short-grain
  white rice
2 cups (500 ml) chicken stock

60 g (2 oz) taleggio, sliced
  (or any other soft oozy cheese,
  such as mozzarella or brie)
2 garlic cloves, extra, sliced
400 g (14 oz) tin cherry tomatoes
1 Lebanese (short) cucumber,
  roughly chopped
3 tablespoons kalamata olives
3 tablespoons chopped dill and
  mint (combined)
1 tablespoon white wine vinegar

OPTIONAL INGREDIENTS
just a resilient atttude if you are
going to make this for a yiayia

IMAGINE AS I WROTE THIS,
I was in a race to finish in time
to eat it. Go.

Preheat the oven to 200°C (400°F).

In an ovenproof frying pan,
fry the onion and zucchini in
1 tablespoon of oil over medium
heat for around 5 minutes, or
until soft but not coloured.

Add the garlic, parsley and kale
and saute for another 5 minutes,
until combined and fragrant.
Season to taste with salt.

Add the butter and rice, and stir
until the rice is fully coated and
the butter has melted. Pour in
the stock and stir.

Put the whole pan in the oven
for 20 minutes.

Place the taleggio on top and
bake for another 5 minutes.

Meanwhile, heat another
tablespoon of oil in a frying pan
over medium–high heat, and

pan-fry the extra garlic for
2 minutes. Add the cherry toms
and cook for another 3 minutes.
This is called a passata party.

Toss together the cucumber,
olives, dill, mint, vinegar and
remaining tablespoon of oil.

Place the garlicky tomatoes and
fresh salad on the baked rice.

Now, just forget the rules.
Scoop and slide.

Hot, sticky, buttery greens rice,
oozing warm taleggio, bouncy
garlicky sweet toms and zingy
bitey herby cold crunch.
It's a hot Greek salad-ish.

Serves 4

Hot Greek Salad-ish

You know when you're craving salad ... but you want it warm, and baked, and saucy, with cheese? Same.

1 small onion, finely chopped
4 garlic cloves, finely chopped
1 tablespoon olive oil
baby fist of oregano leaves
200 g (7 oz) green beans, trimmed
1 teaspoon sea salt
400 g (14 oz) tin crushed tomatoes
rice bran oil, for shallow-frying

FALAFEL MIX*
1½ cups (300 g) dried chickpeas,
   soaked in water overnight
   (or min 2 hours)
½ cup (100 g) dried split fava
   beans, soaked with the
   chickpeas

1 bunch flat-leaf parsley,
   leaves picked
1 bunch mint, leaves picked
3 good handfuls of baby spinach
1 white onion, finely chopped
   (reserve about a quarter of this
   for the salad)
2 garlic cloves, roughly chopped
4 spring onions (scallions), green
   part only, roughly chopped
2 teaspoons ground coriander
1 tablespoon ground cumin
2 tablespoons sea salt,
   or to taste

SALAD
200 g (7 oz) cherry tomatoes,
   halved
handful of flat-leaf parsley leaves
reserved ¼ white onion from
   the falafel
3–4 dill pickles, roughly chopped
1 tablespoon sumac
sea salt and freshly ground
   black pepper

OPTIONAL INGREDIENTS
pita and store-bought dips

IN THE HUNTER VALLEY TOWN where I grew up, my mum shared a garden with a Greek man who, during community market days, would sling these golden delicious medallions hot from a food truck.

I have added tonnes of spinach because it's excellent.

There's no egg either. It's completely vegan, which is something you often hear me say but is so rarely true.

Saute the onion and garlic in the oil over medium heat for 2 minutes, until softened.

Add the oregano, beans and salt and cook for another 3 minutes.

Tip in the tomatoes and cover, then reduce the heat and simmer for 20 minutes.

Meanwhile, make the falafels. Drain the chickpeas and fava beans and tip into the bowl of a food processor. Add the remaining ingredients and blitz until smooth.

Heat about 1 cm (½ inch) of the rice bran oil in a large frying pan over medium–high heat.

Scoop out tablespoons of the falafel mixture and add to the oil in batches. Shallow-fry for about 2 minutes each side until golden.

Remove with a slotted spoon or tongs and drain on paper towel while you cook the rest.

For the salad, toss all the ingredients together in a bowl. Taste and check the seasoning.

Serve while the falafels are hot.

Encourage tearing of bread, swiping of dips, scooping of beans and spoonfuls of salad.

---

*This actually makes about 60 falafels so I like to make and cook half to have with this salad, and freeze the rest of the mix for another time. Any cooked leftovers are great in sambos or salads the next day.

Serves 4–6

Spinach Falafels

The quest for the freshest, crunchiest, herbiest falafels has been cemented into my lizard brain since I was small.

2 tablespoons vegetable oil
1 large red onion, diced
3 garlic cloves, finely chopped
3 cm (1¼ inch) knob of ginger, grated
1 bird's eye chilli, sliced (optional)
1 teaspoon black mustard seeds
2 teaspoons curry powder
2 teaspoons ground turmeric
1 teaspoon garam masala
5 curry leaves
1½ cups (305 g) red split lentils, soaked in water for at least 3 hours

2 cups (500 ml) boiling water
400 ml (13½ fl oz) tin coconut milk
1 small red capsicum (pepper), seeded and diced
100 g (3½ oz) cherry tomatoes

SAMBAL TOPPER
1 cup (65 g) shredded coconut
1 long green chilli, finely chopped
grated zest of 1 lime
3 tablespoons fried shallots
1 tablespoon lime juice
1 teaspoon sea salt

1 teaspoon sesame oil
1 teaspoon chopped coriander (cilantro) stem, leaves reserved for serving

OPTIONAL INGREDIENTS
fried curry leaves and yellow mustard seeds, fried eggs, lime cheeks, roast pumpkin (squash) wedges, baked coconut rice (see page 198) or roti (or homemade flatbread, see page 212)

BREAKING DOWN SPICE RATIOS
of any cuisine and adjusting them to suit your palate is one of the most wonderful parts of cooking.

Daal was basically a unicorn for me. Completely magical, but was it even real? Then I discovered it was and I could make my own.

Soft and aromatic, heavily reliant on warming spices, with threads of heritage to fairytale times.

This one comes via the Fijian ancestry of a friend and uses coconut milk, linking it back to Kerala style.

The scent is heady and perfect for breakfast, lunch, dinner or snacks … and, like my G-rated curry pastes (see page 200), it's a great way to introduce kids to 'spices without heat'.

Heat the oil in a large frying pan over medium heat and saute the onion, garlic, ginger, chilli and mustard seeds for 5 minutes.

Add the curry powder, turmeric, garam masala and curry leaves and cook, stirring, over high heat for 10 minutes.

Drain the lentils and rinse with cold water, then add to the pan and stir well. Pour in the boiling water and bring the whole thing to the boil.

Reduce the heat to low and simmer for 30 minutes, stirring occasionally.

Add the coconut milk, capsicum and tomatoes and simmer, stirring, for 10 minutes.

For the sambal, combine all the ingredients in a bowl.

Spoon the sambal over the daal and finish with the coriander leaves.

Serves 8

Never Daal with Sambal

The concept of mopping up food with another food is the ultimate indulgence for me.

Chicken
Satay

This is a perfect prep-ahead dinner.
You'll just be grilling on the night.

500 g (1 lb 2 oz) chicken
thigh fillets
baked coconut rice
(see page 198), to serve

MARINADE
1 stick lemongrass,
white part only
1 golden shallot, roughly
chopped
3 garlic cloves, roughly chopped
1 tablespoon curry powder
3 tablespoons peanut oil

400 ml (13½ fl oz) tin
coconut milk
1 tablespoon soy sauce
1 tablespoon brown sugar

PEANUT SAUCE
⅔ cup (180 g) peanut butter
1 tablespoon white miso paste
1 teaspoon tamarind paste
2 tablespoons honey
⅔ cup (170 ml) hot water
¼ teaspoon garlic powder
1 tablespoon soy sauce

OPTIONAL INGREDIENTS
lettuce, sliced Lebanese (short)
cucumber, sliced red chilli,
crushed peanuts and lime cheeks

TRUTH BE TOLD, YOU CAN
probably cut out the marinade
if a) you're short of time, or b)
the palates of certain family
members are still partial to the
odd spoonful of playdough.

Yes it adds a layer, but I would
reserve those efforts for when you
have more refined diners to feed.

To make the marinade, blitz the
lemongrass, shallot, garlic and
curry powder in a food processor
until smooth.

Heat 1 tablespoon of the oil in
a frying pan over medium heat,
add the lemongrass paste and
fry for 10 minutes until fragrant.
Add the coconut milk, soy sauce,
brown sugar and remaining oil
and stir until heated through.

Bring to a simmer, then set aside
to cool.

Coat the chicken in the marinade
and leave for at least 2 hours, but
preferably overnight if you can.

To make the peanut sauce, whisk
together all the ingredients in
a large bowl.

When you're ready to cook,
grab some metal skewers and
thread each chicken thigh with
two parallel skewers.

Chargrill the chicken over
medium heat for 7 minutes on
each side or until the chicken
is cooked all the way through.

Remove and rest for 5 minutes,
then slice each chicken thigh
directly between the two
skewers, essentially halving
the chicken popsicle.

Eat with baked coconut rice
and big fat drizzles of the
peanut sauce.

Serves 4

Standby Salads x 3

Either do a single leaf situation or put some effort in. A salad can have
all the opportunities: icy crunch, charred warmth, crispy crumbs, zingy zest.
They're perfect dance partners to a quick grilled meat, or just a solo twirl.

Iceberg Lettuce & Cucumber Salad

1 iceberg lettuce, sliced into 1 cm (½ inch) thick rounds
1 Lebanese (short) cucumber, thinly sliced
3 tablespoons finely chopped dill
3–4 tablespoons grated haloumi
1 tablespoon herb slurry (see page 208)
1 tablespoon white wine vinegar
1 tablespoon olive oil
½ teaspoon sea salt
extra grated haloumi, as a final flourish

Assemble the salad, then dress with herb slurry, vinegar and olive oil, and season with salt. Finish with a scattering of haloumi.

Serves 4–6 as a side

Garbanzo & Tamayto Salad

200 g (7 oz) green beans, trimmed
2 tablespoons olive oil
400 g (14 oz) tin chickpeas, drained and rinsed
2 garlic cloves, sliced
3–4 tablespoons finely chopped oregano
1 tablespoon grated lemon zest
½ teaspoon sea salt
300 g (10½ oz) truss tomatoes, sliced

Sear the green beans in the oil over medium heat for 5 minutes.

Add the chickpeas and garlic and fry on high for 5 minutes.

Assemble everything.

Serves 4–6 as a side

Slaw

2 cups (400 g) corn kernels (fresh or tinned)
1 tablespoon vegetable oil
1 teaspoon sea salt
¼ small cabbage (about 400 g/ 14 oz), shredded
3–4 tablespoons finely chopped chives
1 tablespoon chopped coriander (cilantro), plus extra leaves for serving
1 tablespoon lime juice, plus extra lime for serving
1 tablespoon kewpie mayonnaise
1 tablespoon fried shallots

Fry the corn with the oil and salt until it has a nice char.

Toss everything together and finish with a flurry of coriander leaves. Serve with lime cheeks.

Serves 4–6 as a side

½ cup (40 g) pangrattato
(see page 215)
2 tablespoons finely chopped
woody herb leaves (oregano,
thyme, rosemary)
325 g (11½ oz) cheese ravioli
big handful of baby rocket
(arugula)
2 cups (270 g) shaved zucchini
(courgette) discs, with flowers
if you have them
3 tablespoons marinated
goat's curd

baby fist of mint leaves,
larger leaves shredded
3 tablespoons vinai-no-regrette
(see page 194)
good fist of grated raw haloumi
freshly ground black pepper

OPTIONAL INGREDIENTS
any young fresh herbs or salad
leaves are welcome, as is a
smattering of frozen baby peas,
thawed

THIS CAN'T BE CLASSED AS
a pasta dish or you'd be very
annoyed, but it also loiters
dangerously close to the line
between salad and 'Are you
crazy? That's just macaroni and
cheese made with vinaigrette,
you nut bag.'

It also features my favourite style
of cheese to grate: haloumi.
RAW!

The best thing about this is you
just layer it. Go as many levels up
as you want.

It's a great mid-season dinner but
also a perfect put-together lunch
that goes particularly well with
dappled sunlight and optimism.

Combine the pangrattato with
the woody herbs in a saucepan
over medium heat until just
golden and warmed through.
Set aside.

Boil the ravioli until al dente,
as per the packet instructions.

Scatter the rocket over a platter.

Layer with half the ravioli.

Top with half the zucchini, half the
goat's curd, half the herby crumb
and half the mint. Pour over half
the dressing.

Repeat.

Top with grated raw haloumi and
a good grinding of pepper.

Serves 4

Ravioli
Salad

This falls very neatly into one of those trick salad categories.

1 tablespoon olive oil
600 g (1 lb 5 oz) salmon fillet, skin on, pin-boned
½ cup (125 ml) poke zen dressing (see page 196)
1 avocado, quartered and peeled
2 tablespoons black and white sesame seeds, toasted
¼ cabbage, thinly sliced or shredded (about 4 cups worth)
250 g (9 oz) microwave brown rice
6 radishes, shaved

2 Lebanese (short) cucumbers, shaved
2 spring onions (scallions), green part only, sliced
1 cup (150 g) shelled cooked edamame
1 packet (2 g) crisp seaweed snacks
1 cup (100 g) seaweed salad (store-bought)
2 tablespoons pickled ginger
baby fist of coriander (cilantro) leaves

3–4 x 7-minute boiled eggs*, peeled

OPTIONAL INGREDIENTS
togarashi, furikake, wasabi and kewpie mayonnaise

STARTING WITH A COLD PAN, add the oil then the salmon, skin-side down, and fry over medium heat for 5–7 minutes until the skin is golden.

Flip the salmon over and take the pan off the heat. Allow the residual warmth of the pan to cook it through. I like it medium–rare but you could cook it for another 2 minutes before removing from the heat if you prefer it cooked well.

Let the salmon cool, then remove the skin and break it into bits (you can fry this a little more if it's not crispy enough, then break it up). Cut the flesh into cubes and toss with some of the zen dressing. Keep the rest for drizzling over the salad.

Dunk the sides of the avo in cool water, then dip in the sesame seeds to coat.

Assemble everything else (except the eggs), like a grazing platter.

Right before serving, cut the eggs in half lengthways and place on top.

---

*7-minute eggs work well if you are on a sea level similar to Sydney. Boil water. Eggs from the fridge, prick fat ends with a pin. Lower into water, start timer. Drain, cool slightly and peel. The higher up the mountain, the longer you need to boil the eggs. There is a science here that's just too instructional to add to this book.

Serves 4

Crispy
Salmon
Bowl

This looks intense, but it's just a puzzle really, and we have all done at least one since we were 12, surely?

Chicken Club Salad

There's a no-membership-necessary policy for this club, but this bird has enough bacon to see her VIP'd to covergirl status.

1 kg (2 lb 3 oz) chicken cutlets
  (thighs), bone in, or thigh fillets
olive oil, for brushing
sea salt
150 g (5½ oz) round pancetta,
  thinly sliced
¼ baguette (or ½ small one),
  thinly sliced on the diagonal
2 avocados, peeled and cut into
  wedges or slices
½ iceberg lettuce, cut into
  thin wedges

3 very ripe tomatoes, sliced into
  thin rounds
½ cup (125 ml) vinai-no-regrette
  (see page 194)
2 tablespoons finely chopped
  chives

OPTIONAL INGREDIENTS
fresh bread, to reconstruct into
the stacked sambo you love

I LIKE TO COOK THIS with bone-in cutlets and then, once the chook is done and rested, I cut the bone out and slice the meat. If you find this a little daunting, just ask the butcher to debone the cutlets for you first, or use thigh fillets. Thighs are forgiving (not mine, mind you); you'll just need to reduce the cooking time as explained below.

Preheat the grill function in your oven.

Brush the cutlets or thigh fillets with oil and season with salt. Place, skin-side up, on a baking tray and grill for 5 minutes until crispy.

Switch to oven mode and set to 180°C (350°F).

Cook the chicken cutlets for 10 minutes (if using thigh fillets, skip this bit).

Add the pancetta, softly scrunched or folded in little clusters, to the baking tray with the chicken.

Place the baguette slices onto the tray too, allowing them to soak up the fatty juices.

Return to the oven and roast for a further 20 minutes until the pancetta and bread are crisp and golden, and the cutlets or thigh fillets are cooked through.

Remove from the oven and allow to cool to just warm.

Cut out the bones if you used cutlets, and cut each piece of chicken into about four jaunty slabs. Assemble all the roasted stuff on a platter, along with the avo, icey and tom.

Dress with the vinaigrette and scatter with chives.

Enjoy.

Serves 4–6

2 golden shallots, chunky
  chopped
6 garlic cloves, peeled
  and smashed
1 carrot, chunky chopped
2 tablespoons olive oil
2 sweet potatoes, peeled and
  chunky chopped
2 tablespoons red curry paste
4 cups (1 litre) chicken or
  veg stock
2 teaspoons brown sugar

juice of 2 limes
200 ml (7 fl oz) coconut cream

OPTIONAL INGREDIENTS
coriander (cilantro) leaves
and store-bought roti

WHEN I WAS VISITING my sister in LA, every morning we would visit any number of fancy health-emporiums-come-supermarkets-come-food-barns and buy a basket of treats to consume over the next four hours during our adventures in her Scooby Doo-esque van, until we could settle on somewhere fancy to eat properly and have a martini.

Guaranteed I would get one, if not two, cups of soup with all sorts of accessories thrown on top from the self-serve bar. The luxury of this time seems like a fantasy.

Saute the shallot, garlic and carrot in the olive oil until lightly golden.

Add the sweet potato and curry paste and saute until the edges soften.

Add the stock and simmer for about 25 minutes until the veggies are soft.

Add the brown sugar, lime juice and 150 ml (5 fl oz) of the coconut cream.

Blend until smooth. Use a stick blender if you can or, if using an upright blender, allow to cool first, then reheat to serve. You can add more water if it's too thick.

Serve drizzled with the remaining coconut cream.

You can freeze the leftovers.

Serves 6

Red Curry & Sweet Potato Soup

Soup doesn't have a season.

Tuesday

The week has begun, we have left the gates, everything is unfolding. Have you already dropped the ball? I doubt it. There's little time to check anyway. We want efficient and beautifully delicious.

300 g (10½ oz) cornflour
(cornstarch)
1½ cups (375 ml) soda water
1 tablespoon ground turmeric
2 teaspoons garlic powder
2 teaspoons ground cardamom
1 teaspoon smoked paprika
rice bran oil, for deep-frying
1 whole cauliflower, cut into
small florets
20 mini soft tacos
200 g (7 oz) mozzarella, sliced
into 20 thin rounds

1 cup (250 ml) spicy goddess
(see page 202)

SALSA
250 g (9 oz) cherry tomatoes,
halved
½ red onion, chopped
1 teaspoon sea salt
1 teaspoon sugar
1 teaspoon cumin seeds
1 tablespoon olive oil

CABBAGE SALAD
3 tablespoons lime juice
½ teaspoon ground cumin
¼ red cabbage, shredded
1 teaspoon sea salt

OPTIONAL INGREDIENTS
coriander (cilantro) leaves,
lime wedges, sour cream
and tequila

OVER-STUFFING A TACO IS something I do repeatedly. But like all great things, less is more.

The satisfaction of a hot taco with oozy cheese, crispy cauli, tangy avo sauce and sweet sticky toms is 7500% worth it. A scientific calculation surmised by my six-year-old when asking me how much I like it. Loving it like a motorbike is another measure.

Preheat the oven to 200°C (400°F).

Start with the salsa. Combine all the ingredients in a roasting tin lined with baking paper and pop in the oven for 15 minutes. Set aside and allow to cool, then scoop all the deliciousness into a bowl.

In a large bowl, whisk together the cornflour, soda water, turmeric, garlic powder, cardamom and smoked paprika until it forms a smooth slurry.

Pour 1 cm (½ inch) of oil into a deep frying pan and heat over medium heat. Test the heat with a drip of batter. When it bubbles, you are ready.

Dunk batches of the cauliflower into the batter, allowing the

excess to drip off, then, using tongs, place them in the hot oil. Work in batches so you don't overcrowd the pan.

Fry the cauliflower until golden on each side (about 4 minutes each batch) and place on a wire rack to drain.

This takes a while and gets a little messy with batter drips, but just resign yourself to cleaning it up later.

Once it's all cooked, combine the salad ingredients and let that relax for a bit.

To heat the tacos in cheesy batches, place them on a tray in a single layer with a slice of mozzarella. Then put the tray in the oven until the cheese is oozing.

Serve the tacos hot, like pancakes, on constant rotation from oven to mouth, with the cauli, spicy goddess, salsa and cabbage salad.

If you want to set it all out, just grate the mozz and zap the tacos. No biggie.

Serves the neighbourhood, aka 8–10

Cauli
Tacos

The production of this dish is a splattery, drizzly affair. You may as well have a margarita in hand so the mess is relative.

3 tablespoons Indian curry paste
  (see page 200)
400 g (14 oz) tin crushed
  tomatoes
1 tablespoon brown sugar
400 ml (13½ fl oz) tin
  coconut milk
1 tablespoon sea salt
⅓ cup (50 g) frozen peas
2 handfuls of baby spinach
600 g (1 lb 5 oz) ling or other
  white fish, skin removed
  and pin-boned, sliced into
  3 cm strips

OPTIONAL INGREDIENTS
roti (store-bought or make
it fresh using the flatty dough
on page 212), rice, sliced green
chilli and fried curry leaves

MY KIDS THINK THAT GREEK
yoghurt is akin to ice cream, so
it doesn't take much for us all to
have this with 'ice cream' and
bellies are full.

Fry the curry paste in a large
frying pan over medium–high
heat for 5 minutes, until aromatic
and deeper in colour.

Add the tomatoes and sugar
and simmer for 2 minutes.

Pour in the coconut milk and
simmer for 3 minutes.

Half-fill the tomato tin with water
and swish it about, then add
to the pan, along with the salt.
Simmer for 15 minutes.

Add the peas* and spinach, and
bring back to a simmer.

Add the fish and simmer for
about 3 minutes until just cooked
and tender.

---

*If you are serving little people, hold off
throwing the peas in until you're ready
to serve. They are the ideal little hot-dish
cooler for the kids' bowls.

Serves 4

Fish Curry

This is the perfect antidote to pretty much anything that has already gone wrong this week.

1 tablespoon olive oil
500 g (1 lb 2 oz) pork mince
2 garlic cloves, crushed
½ cup (35 g) shredded coconut
1 cup (200 g) jasmine rice
1 lemongrass end (about 5 cm/
  2 inches), smashed to split
2 makrut lime leaves, roughly torn
3 cups (750 ml) chicken stock

SALAD
1 golden shallot, thinly sliced
1 cup (150 g) cherry tomatoes,
  halved
1 cup (175 g) chopped cucumber
handful of Thai basil leaves
⅓ cup (80 ml) G-rated nuoc
  cham (see page 196)

OPTIONAL INGREDIENTS
pork crackling, fried shallots and
lime wedges

FIRE UP! *CLAP CLAP*. Preheat
the oven to 180°C (350°F).

Place an ovenproof frying pan
over high heat.

Add the oil and mince and fry
until browned (7 minutes).

Add the garlic, coconut and rice
and saute for 3 minutes.

Add the lemongrass, makrut lime
leaves and chicken stock, then
put it in the oven for 20 minutes.

During that 20 minutes make the
salad; aka toss all the ingredients
together with conviction.

Scoop the delicious sticky ricey
larb into bowls and top with the
fresh and cool chopped salad.

Serves 6

Coconut
Rice Larb

Guys, you can get this on the table
in 30 minutes. Here's how.

Red Curry Chicken Meatballs & Sweet Potato Noodles

You can turn this mix into fancy little party sticks, although I'm just not sure I'm ready for that on a Tuesday.

olive oil, for pan-frying
1 bunch Asian greens (gai lan
   or choy sum), cut into 10 cm
   (4 inch) lengths
3 garlic cloves, finely chopped
300 g (10½ oz) sweet potato
   noodles, boiled and drained
my famous dumpling dipping biz
   (1 tablespoon soy sauce,
   1 tablespoon Chinese black
   vinegar and 1 teaspoon
   sesame oil)

MEATBALLS
1 garlic clove, peeled
grated zest and juice of 1 lime
1 golden shallot, finely chopped
1 stick lemongrass, white part
   only, finely chopped
1 makrut lime leaf, shredded
2 tablespoons sesame oil
1 kg (2 lb 3 oz) chicken mince
   (ask your butcher to mince
   some thighs with skin on
   for you – game changer!)
2 tablespoons red curry paste

250 g (9 oz) green beans,
   trimmed and finely chopped
sea salt and freshly ground
   black pepper

OPTIONAL INGREDIENTS
lime wedges and sesame seeds

**LISTEN. YOU, LIKE MY
NEIGHBOUR,** may wish to come
to full blows* with me about the
sweet potato noodles. I like
them. They have the texture
of rubber bands. I remember
chewing rubber bands when
I was little – very satisfying, until
you accidentally swallow one.

Try them once. Decide for
yourself. Change them for another
noodle if you wish. Move on.

For the meatballs, blitz the
garlic, lime zest and juice, shallot,
lemongrass, lime leaf and sesame
oil into a semi-smooth paste.

Combine this with the chicken
mince, red curry paste and
chopped beans, and season
with salt and pepper.

Using a teaspoon, scoop rough
little balls and place on a tray
lined with baking paper. You're
going for about 80 meatballs.
Work out how many you want
to eat (I go about 6 per person),
then freeze the rest on the tray
and bag up once frozen for later.

In a hot, lightly oiled frying
pan over high heat, fry off the
meatballs in batches until nicely
browned, then set aside.

Add the Asian greens and
saute for 2 minutes until slightly
charred, then add the garlic and
fry for a further 5 minutes.

Rinse the cooked noodles under
hot water and add to the pan,
along with the meatballs and the
dipping biz.

Toss the whole lot together well
until the meatballs are cooked
through.

---

*Our 'blows' are often just laughing shock
that we don't agree. Plus, she has a pool,
so we BFF.

*Serves 4, once now, and then
again, and then another time
(makes about 80 meatballs)*

1 cup (180 g) kalamata olives, pitted
1 tablespoon harissa
2 tablespoons tomato paste (concentrated puree)
3 tablespoons olive oil
1.2 kg (2 lb 10 oz) rack of lamb, frenched and cut into 2 equal racks
500 g (1 lb 2 oz) cherry tomatoes
400 g (14 oz) tin cannellini beans, drained and rinsed

2 heads of garlic, halved horizontally
1 kg (2 lb 3 oz) russet or Dutch cream potatoes, peeled and cut into 2 cm pieces
50 g (1¾ oz) butter, chopped
½ cup (130 g) Greek-style yoghurt
sea salt and freshly ground black pepper

OPTIONAL INGREDIENTS
baby spinach and lemon wedges

LAMB CONJURES UP all sorts of memories in our house, from my husband's family farm in New Zealand where they toss shanks to the dogs, to my grandmother's house that smelled of roasting lamb, woody chardonnay and Elizabeth Arden's Red Door, no matter the time of day.

We had off milk in the fridge which led to the revelation that is Greek yoghurt mash.

The perfect zing to go with lamb fat and roast tomatoes.

Preheat the oven to 200°C (400°F).

Blitz the olives, harissa, tomato paste and 2 tablespoons of the oil until smooth, then spread all over the lamb meat.

Heat the remaining oil in a flameproof roasting tin over high heat and sear the lamb, fat-side down, until browned and starting to crisp up.

Set the lamb aside and wipe out any really burnt bits from the tin.

Arrange the tomatoes, beans and garlic in the tin and sit the lamb on top.

Roast for 25–30 minutes if you like your lamb pink, or add another 15 minutes if you prefer it grey. (My grandmother always insisted that perfect doneness was subjective; however, that subjective window was VERY narrow. I inherited this compassionate level of judgery from her.)

Rest the lamb in a warm place for 15 minutes.

While the lamb is roasting, make the mash. Boil the potato in a large saucepan of salted water for 15 minutes or until soft. Drain and return to the pan.

Add the butter and yoghurt and mash to your preferred consistency. Season to taste and keep warm until the lamb is ready.

When you dish up, serve the garlic in whole chunks and let people squeeze the pockets of golden gooey garlic into their dinner, or mouths.

Serves 4–6

Lamb Rack with Harissa, Beans & Yoghurt Mash

This has that lip-smacking, sauce-scooping, salty tang element that I often crave.

½ cup (125 ml) sweet chilli sauce
3 tablespoons soy sauce
2 tablespoons sesame oil
1 kg (2 lb 3 oz) chicken thigh
   fillets, excess fat removed
2 limes, halved
1 bunch basil, leaves picked
1 bunch coriander (cilantro),
   leaves picked

OPTIONAL INGREDIENTS
beer, wraps, a laughter-filled
family reunion

MY BROTHER IS FROM another mother. These are his thighs. Not hers. And actually they're chickens thighs, but his recipe.

He made this when we had a weekend away up north at a sleepy little surf town and reconnected with an arm of our family that has the wit and energy to make you cry with laughter.

Sometime in the afternoon between beers, naked toddler sprinkler dashing and snoozes, the grill was fired up.

It's one of those recipes you can make early or late, for now or tomorrow.

Or just because it's a beach holiday and the grill must go on.

Combine the chilli sauce, soy and sesame oil in a large bowl. Add the chicken and turn to coat, then leave to marinate for 30 minutes.

Heat a large chargrill pan over high heat, or the grill plate on a barbecue. Add the chicken and grill for 5 minutes on each side until cooked through with excellent char lines.

During the last 5 minutes or so, add the lime halves, cut-side down, and let them soften and heat through.

Roughly chop the herbs on a bread board.

Arrange the chicken on the herbs and allow to rest briefly, heating and slightly wilting the herbs.

Carve the chicken into fat slices and serve with the charred limes.

Serves 4

My Brother From Another Mother's Thighs

Take my advice and don't cook this on your own barbecue. Wait till you book an Airbnb and sear the candy marinade onto that one instead.

Saviour Soup x 3

On the run and need a fix? Make a savoury slurp.
These feed two. Or one with a second serve for after or the next day.
My love of soup is a lonesome club at home. Not complaining
when they can be this quick and easy.

Chilli Noodles

2 cups (500 ml) chicken stock
90 g (3 oz) somen noodles
2 handfuls of baby spinach
1 tablespoon chilli paste*
sea salt and freshly ground
  black pepper

Bring the stock to a simmer over
medium–high heat and add the
noodles. Cook for 2 minutes.

Add the spinach and let it wilt.

Stir in the chilli paste, season well
with salt and pepper, and serve.

---

*My favourite is Lao Gan Ma spicy chilli
crisp. It has a cult following, which I urge
you to be part of.

Serves 2

Chorizo & Lentil

50 g (1¾ oz) chorizo, diced
1 roma tomato, diced
½ teaspoon chilli flakes
½ teaspoon dried oregano
2 cups (500 ml) chicken stock
400 g (14 oz) tin lentils, drained
  and rinsed
1 teaspoon tomato paste
  (concentrated puree)
sea salt and freshly ground
  black pepper
big dollop of sour cream

Scatter the chorizo into a cold
deep frying pan, then place over
high heat and sear for 5 minutes
until crispy. Remove and set
aside on a plate.

Add the tomato, chilli and
oregano to the pan and stir.

Add the stock, lentils and tomato
paste and simmer for 10 minutes.

Return the chorizo to the soup,
then taste and season.

Finish with a dollop of sour cream.

Serves 2

Greek Lemon

3 tablespoons jasmine rice
2 cups (500 ml) chicken stock
1 large sprig dill, leaves picked
  and stalk smashed
1 egg
1 teaspoon lemon juice
sea salt and freshly ground
  black pepper

Simmer the rice, stock and dill
stalk for 15 minutes until the
rice is tender (top up with a little
water if needed).

Whisk the egg in a bowl until
pale and foamy, then whisk in
the lemon juice.

Whisk 3 tablespoons of the soup
into the egg mix to temper, then
stir the egg mix back into the
soup. Season to taste.

Top with dill leaves and another
grinding of pepper and eat.

Serves 2

3 tablespoons herb slurry
(see page 208)

TUNA MIX
2 x 185 g (6½ oz) tins tuna
in olive oil, drained
3 tablespoons chopped
flat-leaf parsley
3–4 tablespoons chopped
pickles or cornichons
2 tablespoons finely chopped
red onion
2 teaspoons baby capers,
chopped

3 tablespoons chopped dill
1 tablespoon olive oil
1 teaspoon lemon juice
sea salt and freshly ground
black pepper

SALAD
8 baby potatoes, boiled in
very salty water until tender,
then sliced
250 g (9 oz) green beans,
tails trimmed, blanched
4 tomatoes, sliced

4 x 7-minute eggs*, peeled and
halved lengthways
2 baby cos lettuces, trimmed,
washed and quartered

OPTIONAL INGREDIENTS
a smug outlook, considering
you've maintained some bowl
goals this far into the week

**THIS IS SUCH A GREAT 'WORK'
SALAD.** Make it in a lunchbox
like this: potatoes, beans,
tomatoes first, then herb
slurry. Top with tuna mix, then
the lettuce and a whole egg.
If you do it in this order, the
lettuce will stay crisp. You'll
be so impressed with yourself
you'll want to deliberately walk
around the office munching on
it, interrupting casual meetings
and pointing at things with your
fork while you chat until someone
sparks up, 'Oooh, what have
you got today?' or 'That looks
great, who made it?' yada yada.
Don't do this. You are eating egg
and tuna. It's the greatest office
offence after #metoo.

For the tuna mix, combine all the
ingredients in a bowl.

Same for the salad ingredients.

Divide the salad and tuna mix
among four bowls and drizzle
with the herb slurry.

*7-minute eggs work well if you are on
a sea level similar to Sydney. Boil water.
Eggs from the fridge, prick fat ends with
a pin. Lower into water, start timer. Drain,
cool slightly and peel. The higher up the
mountain, the longer you need to boil the
eggs. There is a science here that's just too
instructional to add to this book.

Serves 4

Tinned Tuna Nicoise Salad

Despite my disparaging comments opposite, this is definitely a workday lunch solution waiting to happen.

1 whole chicken (doesn't matter
what size, but I tend to veer
towards 1.2 kg/2 lb 10 oz),
spine removed, pressed flat*

SAUCE
½ cup (125 ml) soy sauce
3 tablespoons honey
5 cm (2 inch) knob of ginger,
peeled and left whole
3 spring onions (scallions), white
parts roughly chopped, green
tops reserved for garnish**

1 onion, quartered
6 garlic cloves, peeled
and smashed
3 tablespoons Chinese
black vinegar
1 tablespoon chilli bean paste
1 tablespoon chicken stock
powder

NOODLES
2 tablespoons olive oil
2 bunches water spinach, cut
into 10 cm (4 inch) pieces

6 garlic cloves, sliced
500 g (1 lb 2 oz) fresh rice
noodles (or use dry noodles
cooked according to the
packet instructions)
1 tablespoon sesame oil

OPTIONAL INGREDIENTS
nothing, not even paper towel,
is essential here

I TRULY BELIEVE THAT NONE
of you read the name of this
recipe without adding the defiant
and forceful enunciation of
a rapper. It just happens. And
if it didn't, I bet it has now.

Preheat the oven to 200°C
(400°F).

Warm all the sauce ingredients
with ½ cup (125 ml) of water in
a saucepan.

Put the chicken in a deep baking
dish lined with baking paper and
pour the sauce over the top.

Place in the oven for 45 minutes.
I put a piece of foil over mine at
about 25 minutes as the skin was
really taking that self tan too far!
Not tight, just literally rest the foil
on the top. Untucked.

While that's happening, get the
noodles ready. In a large frying
pan over medium heat, add the
oil and cook the spinach and
garlic slivers until the garlic just
starts to brown.

Add the rice noodles and
3 tablespoons of water to loosen
them. Toss this well and dress
with the sesame oil.

Cut the chicken into pieces to
serve. (The hardest bit is the
thigh bone, but you can leave
this whole if you like. Everything
else you can snip at the joint.)

Slice the now candied ginger
to serve on top (do not rob your
guests of this incredible accent!),
along with the curly green tops of
the spring onions.

*This is a big ask for a Tuesday, I know, but
I like to think that appreciating the food
we eat extends beyond simply knowing an
ingredient to the handling of it (although
I grew up on a working farm so I have had
the benefit of experience from a young
age). But if it's not for you, just ask your
butcher to do this for you.

**Finely slice the green spring onion tops
lengthways or on a very sharp angle and
put in a glass of iced water so they curl up.
Completely unnecessary when it comes to
flavour but such a fun accessory.

Serves 4–6

Shandong Chicken

Every comfort food dish in every country ultimately comes down to carbs'n'sauce.

400 g (14 oz) piece of BBQ pork
with sauce

200 g (7 oz) rice noodles, cooked
according to the packet
instructions

1 cup (140 g) pickled carrot (see
page 196), plus 2 tablespoons
of the brine

500 g (1 lb 2 oz) iceberg lettuce,
shredded

2 Lebanese (short) cucumbers,
sliced into random pointy
spears

3 tablespoons coriander
(cilantro) leaves

3 tablespoons thinly sliced
spring onion (scallion)

2 tablespoons fried shallots

1 tablespoon sesame oil

2 teaspoons Maggi seasoning

OPTIONAL INGREDIENTS
chilli

THERE'S A BANH MI JOINT not far from my studio, which uses freshly baked bread rolls that are super crispy out and fluffy in. People queue down the street for them.

But the line moves fast. The pace at which they assemble a sandwich and the stare of fury if you falter with your order once you reach the counter keeps things rolling.

The chilli is so hot here that I ask if they wouldn't mind just waving it past the sandwich. (This often means I end up with a malicious teaspoonful dumped in at the last minute.)

What makes this flavour combo so iconic is the pickled carrot and the Maggi seasoning sauce. This crazy little dropper bottle of umami is strangely nondescript. It's found all over south-east Asia on DIY condiment islands, although a Google search told me it was created in Switzerland, which I was NOT expecting. You could spend less time assembling this salad than I spent researching this.

That said, if you don't have it, sub it out with 50:50 soy and Worcestershire.

This is all assembly, and should be done just before serving.

Preheat the oven to 200°C (400°F).

Wrap the pork in foil and warm slightly in the oven for 10 minutes or so. (Or don't wrap it in foil and heat it in the microwave.) Thinly slice the meat. Keep the sauce!

Put together on a platter with the noodles, carrot, lettuce and cucumber. I like to keep the ingredients in sections so people can pick their bits.

Top with the coriander, spring onion and fried shallots and drizzle with sesame oil, Maggi seasoning, the carrot brine and the pork sauce.

Serves 4

Char Sui Bún Salad

My favourite sambo as a salad?
Yes please.

Silky
Soup

This is the kind of soup that I imagine eating while wearing velour sweats when I retire. This soup and martinis

1 tablespoon olive oil
50 g (1¾ oz) butter
1 leek, white and pale green
    part only, cut into 1 cm
    (½ inch) thick slices
2 parsnips, peeled and
    roughly chopped
1 head of cauliflower,
    roughly chopped
2 zucchini (courgettes),
    roughly chopped
1 head of garlic, halved
    horizontally

1 litre (34 fl oz) chicken stock
sea salt and freshly ground
    black pepper

CRUNCHY TOPPING
3 tablespoons olive oil
2 tablespoons baby capers,
    patted as dry as possible
½ cup (30 g) fresh breadcrumbs

OPTIONAL INGREDIENTS
herb slurry (see page 208)

LIKE EATING A CLOUD DREAM.

Low carb (if that's your thing)
but rich and seemingly full of
cream. It'd be pretty easy to veg
or veganise this too.

Heat the oil and butter in a large
saucepan over medium heat.

When the butter has melted,
add the leek, parsnip, cauliflower,
zucchini and garlic head and
cook for 15 minutes until the
vegetables are starting to soften.

Add the stock and simmer for
30 minutes.

Remove the garlic and squeeze
the soft flesh back into the soup.

Blitz. Season to taste.

For the topping, heat the oil in
a large frying pan until hot and
add the capers.

These will spit and generally
behave badly so keep an eye
on them.

Once they blossom open
crisply or begin to brown, add
the breadcrumbs and continue to
fry, stirring, until golden brown.

Eat the soup with a handful of
crumbs and capers on top.

Serves 4

1.5 kg (3 lb 5 oz) beef rump, trimmed and thinly sliced
2 tablespoons rice bran oil
2 cm (¾ inch) knob of ginger, peeled and sliced into thin strips
3 spring onions (scallions), roughly chopped
450 g (1 lb) fresh rice sheet noodles, at room temperature, cut into discs (or regular fresh rice noodles)

100 g (3½ oz) water spinach, chopped into 5 cm (2 inch) lengths
140 g (5 oz) snow peas (mange tout), topped, tailed and halved
6 garlic cloves, sliced
1 tablespoon sesame oil

MARINADE
1 cup (250 ml) kecap manis
½ cup (125 ml) soy sauce
½ cup (125 ml) oyster sauce

½ cup (125 ml) Chinese black vinegar
3 tablespoons sesame oil
8 garlic cloves, crushed
10 cm (4 inch) knob of ginger, peeled and grated
2 spring onions (scallions), finely chopped

OPTIONAL INGREDIENTS
sesame seeds

I HAVE LEARNED THE HARD WAY that my wok is not big enough and my hotplate not fierce enough for all the stirring and frying to happen at the same time, inevitably ending in a stewed, tough, confusing dish.

So here is the go.

Cook all the bits separately, in an order that means the thing you want hottest is last in the pan, then put it in a bowl and stir it there.

Combine the marinade ingredients in a large container. I have tricked you into prepping ahead because this will make twice as much as you need. You have options here. You can:

(a) be mad

(b) store the rest in the fridge for something later (prawns, barbecued chicken, baked wings)

(c) just halve the quantities.

Coat the beef in half the marinade and leave overnight or for at least an hour, which occasionally means 15 minutes on rushed nights at my house.

Heat a splash of oil in a large non-stick frying pan over high heat and fry the ginger, spring onion and noodles for 5 minutes. Set aside in a large serving bowl.

Add more oil if needed and fry the water spinach, snow peas and garlic for 5 minutes.

Place this on top of the noodles.

Add a little more oil and fry the beef in batches (reserving the marinade) over the highest possible heat for 2 minutes each side until just cooked through. Place the meat directly on the vegetables.

Once all the beef is cooked, reduce the heat, add the reserved marinade to the pan and bring to a simmer. Pour this over the meat, vegetables and noodles, toss together and drizzle with sesame oil.

Serves 4

Marinated Seared Beef

This has the essence of a stir-fry, without actually being one.

Wednesday

If you're anything like me, today is the day you start to wonder what day it actually is, and I find the 'hump day' label is far less invigorating than it should be. Is it really only Wednesday? I start to cook with an extra dash of laziness at this point. It tastes great.

3 potatoes (big, fat and dirty),
  boiled until tender, peeled
5 eggs
½ cup (125 ml) single
  (pure) cream
1 onion, thinly sliced
⅓ cup (80 ml) olive oil
2 small zucchini (courgettes),
  thinly sliced
1 tablespoon sea salt
1 tablespoon chilli flakes
1 tablespoon chopped oregano

1 tablespoon chopped thyme
⅓ cup (80 g) goat's curd
large handful of grated
  or sliced mozzarella

OPTIONAL INGREDIENTS
asparagus or salad

EVERY TIME I MAKE THIS, my ambition is to be transported to the counter at Flour and Stone in Sydney, where (along with all sorts of other divine baked goods) they sell a zucchini, chilli, cheese folded-over bun thing. This is not a bun, but it's like wearing a shirt instead of a skirt in a similar print, capeesh?

Preheat the oven to 180°C (350°F).

Roughly break up the potatoes into chunks.

Whisk the eggs and cream together.

Pan-fry the onion slices in 2 tablespoons of oil over low heat until soft. (You could do this in the pan you intend to bake in to save the kids some washing up.)

In a low-sided baking tin (about 35 cm x 25 cm/14 inch x 10 inch) or a flameproof casserole dish, toss the potato chunks with the remaining oil, the zuke, onion (with its oil), salt, chilli flakes, oregano and thyme.

Pour the egg and cream mixture over the top.

Position little dumplings of goat's curd over the top and then cover haphazardly with mozzarella.

Bake for 30 minutes.

It can be eaten cold, but if you get it warm, time stops.

Serves 6

Frittato
with
Zucchini

Never overthink the composition
of dishes containing egg, potato
and cream. It's bound to end well.

250 g (9 oz) beef mince
3 tablespoons olive oil,
    plus extra for drizzling
1 onion, chopped
2 teaspoons sea salt
1 tablespoon chopped oregano
2 garlic cloves, crushed
1 cup (160 g) frozen spinach
1⅓ cups (310 g) fresh ricotta
½ teaspoon lemon zest
16 large pasta shells
1¼ cups (310 g) tomato passata
    (pureed tomatoes)

1½ cups (190 g) grated
    mozzarella
½ teaspoon chilli flakes

OPTIONAL INGREDIENTS
rocket salad

STUFFING SOMETHING IN PASTA
shells and topping with oozing
cheese has the same culinary
effect on most kids as crumbing
and frying.

It could be playdough or
something worse and they'd
still eat it.

I won't pretend I am beyond this
adolescent weakness.

This has mince but also a good
whack of spinach, which would
be hard for the fussiest to dissect
without tweezers.

Preheat the oven to 180°C
(350°F).

Fry the mince in 1 tablespoon of
oil over high heat for 7 minutes
or so until browned, breaking up
any large clumps as you go.

Add the onion, 1 teaspoon of salt
and 1 tablespoon of oil and saute
for 5 minutes.

Add the oregano and 1 teaspoon
of garlic and cook for 5 minutes.

Add the spinach (it's OK if it's still
frozen) and saute until thawed.
Set aside to cool.

Once cooled, combine the mince
mixture with the ricotta and
lemon zest.

Meanwhile, cook the pasta shells
until they are just al dente. Drain.

In the base of an ovenproof
frying pan (the one you fried
in, perhaps?) or a baking dish,
place the tomato passata and
the remaining garlic, oil and salt.
Mix together well.

Stuff each pasta shell with
2 tablespoons of the mince and
ricotta filling.

Nestle the shells snugly into the
tomato sauce.

Top with the mozzarella and chilli
flakes and finish with a good
drizzle of oil.

Bake in the oven for 15 minutes,
or until you have a golden,
bubbling mess.

Serves 4

Stuffed Shells

Seriously, what's not to love here?

450 g (1 lb) Dutch carrots,
   halved lengthways
400 g (14 oz) tin chickpeas,
   drained and rinsed
3 tablespoons honey
8 sprigs thyme
1 x 1.5 kg (3 lb 5 oz) chicken,
   spine removed, flattened
50 g (1¾ oz) butter, melted
   and kept hot
1 tablespoon sea salt
1 tablespoon olive oil

OPTIONAL INGREDIENTS
green salad and lemon cheeks

I LIKE SECTIONING the chook along one side of the spine (or both if I want to be rid of the zipper-like column altogether) and then cracking the breast plate against a flat surface.

I appreciate that this sounds very brutal, but you can always distract yourself and consider some year 5 maths equations.

It's satisfying learning a few little butchery skills and I think in a way it pays a little homage to the animal that will imminently sustain you.

But of course, if you really just don't want to, then ask your local butcher to do it for you when you buy it.

Preheat the oven to 180°C (350°F).

Toss together the carrots, chickpeas, honey and thyme in a roasting tin.

Place the flattened chook on top, skin-side up, in the middle of the tin.

Pour the hot butter evenly over the chicken and then sprinkle with the salt.

Pour the oil and ⅔ cup (160 ml) of water over the veg.

Roast for 45 minutes or until the chicken is cooked through.

You can pierce the thigh meat to see if the juices run clear, but somehow this always results in dry meat for me. Buying a meat thermometer is the best way until you have a good instinct for these things, or a hardy layer of salmonella has built up in your family's gut lining.

Once out of the oven, allow the chook to rest in the tin with the veg for about 15 minutes while you assess the possibilities of salad, wine and a relaxing family dinner.

Serves 4–6

Flat Roast Chook with Honey Carrots & Chickpeas

Flattening a chook is a crunchy affair. And less confronting than you might think.

6 chicken cutlets (thighs,
  about 1 kg/2 lb 6 oz)
3 tablespoons Thai curry paste
  (see page 200)
200 ml (7 fl oz) coconut cream
1 cup (250 ml) chicken stock
2 tablespoons lime juice
1 tablespoon fish sauce
2 tablespoons brown sugar
200 g (7 oz) green beans,
  trimmed and halved
½ cup (125 g) bamboo shoots,
  thinly sliced

OPTIONAL INGREDIENTS
basil leaves, lime wedges,
sliced chilli and rice

**REMEMBER DINNER AT YOUR
LOCAL THAI** joint with your
friends and a bottle of savvy b
on a Wednesday?

The sophistication was almost
too much to bear.

But summer in the 90s is a fond
place to return to, and all I need
(aside from astringent plonk) is a
nightclub destination that serves
free-pour vodka sodas and allows
smoking indoors.

The fact that the G-ness of this
curry means kids can eat it also
means that I may well be wearing
some of it (kids + soupy stuff =
ridiculous) before the idea of
midweek late-night dancing
can even be considered.

Place the chicken cutlets,
skin-side down, in a large cold
frying pan, then cook over
medium–high heat for 5 minutes.
Turn them over and cook for
another 10 minutes. Transfer
the chicken to a plate.

Remove all but 1 tablespoon
of the rendered fat in the pan.
(Keep this stuff for literally any
beauty regime you can imagine
incorporating it into, or frying
eggs, or potatoes, or pasta!)

Add the curry paste to the pan
and cook, stirring, for 2 minutes
until fragrant.

Pour in the coconut cream and
stock, reduce the heat to medium
and simmer for 5 minutes.

Add the lime juice, fish sauce
and sugar. Taste and adjust if the
flavours need balancing.

Place the beans, bamboo shoots
and chicken on top and simmer
for 10 minutes until the chicken
is cooked through. Go.

Serves 4–6

G-rated
Red Chicken
Curry

Flashbacks now occur on Wednesdays.

Tandoori Chops & Rainbow Jewel Salad

No unicorns were harmed in the making of this dinner.

3 tablespoons tandoori paste
3 tablespoons plain yoghurt
12 lamb chops, frenched
a bunch of pappadums, some
  whole, some broken to crunch
  into the salad
1 baby cos lettuce, leaves
  separated

ROAST CAULIFLOWER
600 g (1 lb 5 oz) cauliflower,
  cut into florets

1 onion, sliced
2 tablespoons rice bran oil
10 curry leaves
2 teaspoons mustard seeds
  (black and yellow)
2 teaspoons curry powder
1 teaspoon sea salt
3 tablespoons mango chutney
1 tablespoon lime juice

JEWELS
1 Lebanese (short) cucumber,
  diced (emeralds)
½ red capsicum (pepper),
  seeded and diced (rubies)
2–3 radishes, sliced (giant crown
  jewels, or lovely rose quartz)
1 carrot, diced (garnet)

OPTIONAL INGREDIENTS
lime wedges and plain yoghurt

A FEW YEARS AGO I told someone who was wasting my time that cubed vegetables were coming back. And now here we are. Cubing like a ninja.

Combine the tandoori paste and yoghurt in a glass or ceramic bowl, add the lamb chops and toss to coat.

These should wallow in this sump of deliciously pungent paste for a couple of hours, or at the very least 20 minutes. (If you've never marinated with a pigment-strong spice in brand new Tupperware, then you may as well do it now. You will only ever do it once.)

Preheat the oven to 180°C (350°F).

For the roast cauliflower, toss together the cauliflower, onion, oil, curry leaves, mustard seeds, curry powder and salt. Spread out on a lined baking tray and roast for 20 minutes.

Take the roast cauliflower out of the oven and toss through the mango chutney and lime juice. Set aside to cool.

Grill the chops over high heat. This is best done outside, downwind from the washing line if you can. If not, I would actually put them under an oven grill (broiler), rather than attempt stove-top chargrilling, as the iridescently red paste will spit and splatter in a very aggressive fashion. About 3 minutes each side will do it, then remove and rest.

Add the jewel vegetables to the cooling cauli and toss again.

Eat the chops and cauli salad with smashed and whole puppies and crisp little cos leaves.

Serves 4

1 tablespoon olive oil
1 large leek, white and pale green parts only, chopped
100 g (3½ oz) streaky bacon, cut into 1 cm (½ inch) pieces
25 g (1 oz) butter
1 tablespoon tarragon leaves, roughly chopped
200 g (7 oz) mushrooms*, cut into 1 cm (½ inch) pieces
500 g (1 lb 2 oz) roast chook, shredded**

2 tablespoons plain (all-purpose) flour
200 g (7 oz) creme fraiche
1 tablespoon chicken stock powder
sea salt and freshly ground black pepper
1 rectangular sheet (or 2 squares) good-quality puff pastry
1 egg

OPTIONAL INGREDIENTS
peas, mushy or whole

YOUR PIE OF CHOICE might have a soft base, and a top so flaky that inhaling while eating is life threatening.

It may very well be a crunchy base (said no one ever).

For me, it's crispy layers on the top gently meeting the filling, then, of course, the sauce.

Usually eaten in the car, whatever the filling is, it's just a carriage for the rich sauce to viscously piggy-back on between bites, instead of falling into my lap and searing my thighs even through denim.

Until now.

These days I gleefully eat pie from a bowl with whatever ratio I want of pastry (soft OR flaky), chunky stuff and gravy!

Preheat the oven to 180°C (350°F).

Heat the oil in an ovenproof frying pan or a flameproof casserole dish over medium heat. Add the leek and bacon and saute for 8 minutes or until nicely softened.

Add the butter, tarragon and mushroom and stir well, then reduce the heat to low and pop the lid on for 10 minutes.

This is a wet fry for the mushrooms, guys. The best way to get that delicious sauce flavour but keep them plump and juicy.

Add the chook and flour and stir well, then add the creme fraiche, stock powder and 1 cup (250 ml) of water. Stir again. Put the lid back on and simmer for a further 10 minutes. Taste and season.

Strain, keeping both the chicken mixture and the liquid!

Spoon the chicken mix into the centre of the pan and cover with the pastry, tucking it around the side, sealing the edges.

Depending on my level of hunger, I will either scrunch and jam the corners of the pastry around the edge and sometimes under the pie filling, à la teenager making a bed, OR I will trim the pastry so there is enough to tuck the filling in firmly, then set about with the intention of decorating

my pie with the rest … twisting perimeter ropes are nice and cook well.

Cut a steam hole in the middle of the pastry lid. Whisk the egg with 1 tablespoon water and brush over the pastry.

Bake for 20 minutes until puffed and golden.

Heat the reserved liquid (which should have thickened from the flour, but not to the gelatinous extent that would pass an inspection by the CWA***) to DIY to your own slice of pie.

---

*Use any you like, but a Swiss brown is lovely and subtle with enough flavour to warrant its existence. It also holds its button shape, and contains its grey colour rather than bleeding into the sauce too much.

**Store-bought BBQ chook is great for this, but you can actually use any cooked cut you like.

***Said in envious jest, as this is quite clearly a club I will never make the cut for. Baking is possibly the only science I get a bit flat-earthy about because it just defies logic.

Serves 6

Side of Sauce with Chicken Pie

Growing up in a country town, you get to know the local pie, and this will dictate your preferences forever.

Midweek Rump

Who can turn down
a midweek rump?

4 pieces lamb rump (1.4 kg/
    3 lb 1 oz), cap trimmed,
    but ask for a sliver of fat
    to remain
500 g (1 lb 2 oz) baby potatoes,
    boiled until tender, drained
1 tablespoon lemon juice
2 tablespoons olive oil
3 tablespoons rosemary leaves
4 garlic cloves, peeled and
    smashed
1 small onion, sliced

500 g (1 lb 2 oz) frozen
    baby peas
1 teaspoon sea salt
1 teaspoon sugar
baby fist of mint leaves

OPTIONAL INGREDIENTS
gravy

I AM GOING TO TYPE this quick so you can slip into something comfortable and get to the good stuff faster.

Preheat the oven to 220°C (425°F).

Place the lamb, fat-side down, in a flameproof baking dish while it is cold* and then place over medium–high heat to sear for 10 minutes.

You won't need oil. A lot of fat will render off.

Remove the dish from the heat and transfer the lamb to a plate.

Tear or light smash the baby spuds and toss in the dish with the lemon juice, 1 tablespoon of oil, rosemary, garlic and onion.

Nestle the lamb on top of the spuds.

Place the dish in the oven for 20 minutes, then remove and let it rest for 10 minutes while you make the minty peas.

Blanch the peas.

Blitz half the peas with the salt, sugar, mint and remaining oil in a food processor, or just mash with a fork (in which case you'll need to chop the mint).

Toss with the whole peas.

Carve the lamb into 1 cm (½ inch) thick slices and serve with all those incredible accessories.

---

*The trick of the cold pan is that all the meat fat will have pan-contact, instead of curling away from the searing heat, leaving you with an uneven brown.

Serves 6

Panic Pastas x 3

Sophia Loren was right … I can immediately tell when I need to thank spaghetti for my figure. I find it more than a little unjust that the carbohydrate does not choose to blossom under my skin in the way it so clearly does with hers. Perhaps it would help if I perfected a sultry Italian accent.

Meatball Ziti

4 pork and fennel sausages
1 tablespoon olive oil
330 g (11½ oz) tomato passata
   (pureed tomatoes)
baby fist of basil leaves
200 g (7 oz) ziti pasta
sea salt and freshly ground
   black pepper
handful of grated parmesan

Remove the skins from the
sausages and cut them into
bite-sized chunks.

Pan-fry in the oil over medium
heat for 10 minutes, until golden.

Add the passata and basil leaves,
and simmer for 5 minutes.

Meanwhile, cook the ziti until al
dente, then drain, reserving about
3 tablespoons of the pasta water.

Add the ziti and pasta water to
the sausage mixture and toss
to combine.

Season and top with cheese.

Serves 2

Mini (stuff) Max (flavour)

200 g (7 oz) shell pasta
1 tablespoon olive oil,
   plus extra for drizzling
3 garlic cloves, chopped
baby fist of flat-leaf parsley
   leaves, chopped
2 anchovies, chopped
1 tablespoon lemon juice
sea salt and freshly ground
   black pepper
¼ teaspoon chilli flakes

Cook the pasta until al dente,
then drain, reserving about
3 tablespoons of the pasta water.

Meanwhile, heat the oil in a frying
pan over medium heat and saute
the garlic, parsley and anchovy
until the garlic is just golden,
about 5 minutes. Don't let it burn
or it will taste bitter.

Stir in the lemon juice.

Add the pasta and reserved
pasta water and toss to combine.
Season with salt and pepper.

Finish with the chilli flakes and
a big drizzle of olive oil.

Serves 2

Carb Carbonara

3 eggs, plus 2 egg yolks
1 tablespoon freshly ground
   black pepper
1½ cups (150 g) grated
   parmesan
200 g (7 oz) streaky bacon,
   cut into thin strips
200 g (7 oz) spaghetti

Whisk together the eggs, extra
yolks, pepper and parmesan.

Fry the bacon over medium heat
until crispy. Remove to a plate,
leaving the fat in the pan.

Meanwhile, cook the spaghetti
until al dente, then drain,
reserving about ½ cup (125 ml)
of the pasta water.

Add the reserved water to the
bacon fat in the pan and bring
to a simmer.

Add the spaghetti and stir well.

Remove the pan from the heat
and slowly add the egg mixture,
stirring constantly. Return the
bacon and keep stirring until
the sauce is glossy and coats
every last strand of spaghetti.
Eat immediately.

Serves 2

2 kg (4 lb 6 oz) chicken wings*

MARINADE
½ cup (125 ml) soy sauce
3 tablespoons Chinese
   black vinegar
3 tablespoons sesame oil
½ cup (175 g) honey
6 cm (2½ inch) knob of
   ginger, sliced
8 spring onions (scallions), green
   tops reserved for garnish
1 head of garlic, halved
   horizontally

OPTIONAL INGREDIENTS
sesame seeds and jasmine rice

WINGS THIS STICKY are perfect for lick/suck/chucking. Best eaten with people who already love you.

Preheat the oven to 220°C (425°F).

Place all the marinade ingredients in a large baking dish and warm it in the oven for a few minutes.

This is just to make the honey easier to blend with everything else. It should only be just warm.

Toss the wings into this beautiful mess and coat well.

Cover the dish with baking paper and then tightly with foil.

Bake for 40 minutes, then remove the foil and paper and turn the wings. Finish baking uncovered for another 20 minutes.

These should be so tender you can just suck the flesh from every bone like a reckless giant and fling the scraps over your shoulder. There is no other way.

---

*I remove the tips because this candy land will just burn them. Instead, throw those offcuts in a pot with some soup basics and make yourself a broth.

Serves 6

Sticky
Wings

I strongly feel that if the Rolling Stones had to reshoot the album cover for Sticky Fingers they would opt for a close-up of this hot mess.

500 g (1 lb 2 oz) linguine
400 g (14 oz) raw prawn meat
4 garlic cloves, chopped
1 bird's eye chilli, chopped
handful of curly parsley leaves,
   finely chopped
⅓ cup (80 ml) olive oil
100 g (3½ oz) butter
100 ml (3½ fl oz) lemon juice
sea salt and freshly ground
   black pepper

OPTIONAL INGREDIENTS
rocket (arugula) leaves

IF PRAWN LINGUINE is printed on a menu, it's Saturday lunchtime and you are dining with friends, I can almost guarantee you should text the babysitter now and ask how much later they can really stay after the agreed time.

If it is in fact a Wednesday when you are making this, then you are already checking out of the work week and into the weekend. You should text people now and make some plans.

Cook the pasta until al dente (usually 8 minutes for dry linguine). I like to time this so that I can tong the cooked pasta straight into the prawns*. So as soon as you set that water on to boil, get busy with the prawns.

Finely chop the prawn meat into roughly 5 mm (⅛ inch) rounds.

In a large deep saucepan (big enough to hold the cooked pasta comfortably), pan-fry the garlic, chilli and parsley in 2 tablespoons of oil over high heat for 5 minutes.

Add the prawn meat and let it react (it'll blush a bit and become white) for 2 minutes. Add the butter and let it foam for 1 minute.

You can add the pasta now, along with the lemon juice and remaining oil. Season to taste.

Give it a good sloosh sloosh. If you went your own way and drained the pasta instead of tonging it, add a big slurp of the pasta water you remembered to save to loosen everything up.

---

*If you don't, please make sure to scoop out a cup of pasta water before draining. You'll need some at the end.

Serves 4

Prawn
Linguine

All day dreaming of the weekend.
Are we there yet?

1 teaspoon olive oil
1 chicken breast fillet
  (around 220 g/8 oz)
8 frozen dumplings
  (see page 130)
180 g (6½ oz) somen noodles
2 tablespoons tom yum paste
400 ml (13½ fl oz) tin
  coconut milk
2 heads of bok choy
1 teaspoon sesame oil
1 tablespoon lime juice

1–2 teaspoons chilli paste

OPTIONAL INGREDIENTS
noise-cancelling headphones

AT SOME POINT EVERY WEEK
I completely lose track of time.
This happens so commonly on
a Wednesday that it should act
as a reliable time stamp.

There's always someone at
some kind of sport practice and
usually a child in the house who
belongs to another family in the
neighbourhood.

It's a comfortingly confusing day,
Wednesday.

Mainly because there are
often leftovers for the kids
from yesterday, which means a
compilation dinner of spices and
flavours, dumplings, and some
vegetables, blossoming and
undisguised. The world is your
drunken (somewhere between
soup and sauce) bowl.

Just the way a Wednesday
should be.

Preheat the oven to 200°C (400°F).

Heat the oil in a large ovenproof
frying pan over high heat and
pan-fry the chicken breast for
2 minutes each side. Place in the

oven for a few minutes to finish
cooking through.

Boil the dumplings for 1 minute
or until thawed. Add the somen
noodles and cook according to
the packet instructions. Drain.

Remove the pan from the
oven and set the chicken aside.
Fry the tom yum paste over
medium–high heat for 2 minutes,
then pour in the coconut milk.
Add ½ cup (125 ml) of water
to the tin and swish it around,
then add to the pan. Bring to
a simmer, stirring to combine
with the tom yum paste.

Meanwhile, lightly steam the
bok choy.

Slice the chicken and divide
among two shallow bowls, then
add the noodles, dumplings and
bok choy.

Pour the broth over the top.
Drizzle with sesame oil, then the
lime juice and top with as much
chilli paste as you can handle.

Serves 2

Drunken Dumplings

For when you can't commit to the idea
of either a soup or a stir-fry.

2 cups (500 ml) milk
4 cups (1 litre) beshy
(see page 204)
200 g (7 oz) Red Leicester
cheese, grated
200 g (7 oz) cheddar, grated
100 g (3½ oz) mozzarella,
grated
1 small cauliflower, cut into
1 cm (½ inch) thick slices,
big bits snapped into chunks
2 corn cobs, kernels removed,
cobs reserved

sea salt and freshly ground
black pepper
500 g (1 lb 2 oz) macaroni
2 tablespoons olive oil
2 leeks, white and pale green
parts only, sliced into 5 mm
(⅛ inch) thick rounds
½ teaspoon sweet paprika

OPTIONAL INGREDIENTS
a Stable Table – you can
simultaneously insult and impress
people if you buy them one

THE STANDARD PASTA pack size of 500 g (1 lb 2 oz) is just so perfectly designed to make you use it all. It's a lovely generous amount to deal with; you always think to yourself, 'the kids can eat what we don't use tonight with sausages tomorrow'. And it absolutely does not matter if you have used EXACTLY half a packet one day – when you need a half packet from the pantry on another day you are adamant that it's under and won't be enough.

Genius mind mastery to the person who did this!

Preheat the oven to 180°C (350°F).

Stir the milk into the bechamel in a saucepan over medium heat until hot. Add the grated cheeses, a handful at a time, making sure the last lot has melted before you add the next. Keep warm once it's all melted in.

Place the cauli in a colander, and sit the colander in a big stainless steel bowl.

Put the corn cobs in a big saucepan filled with 20 cups (5 litres) of water and a heaped tablespoon of salt and bring to the boil. Cook the pasta in this corny water for 1 minute less than the packet instructions suggest for al dente.

DRAIN THE PASTA OVER THE CAULIFLOWER. Discard the corn cobs and allow the cauliflower and pasta to steam for a minute before releasing the water.

Use 1 tablespoon of oil to grease the base of a large baking dish and fill with the pasta, cauliflower, corn kernels and leek. Toss it all to combine and season well.

Pour the cheese beshy over the pasta mix, gradually allowing it to sink in and settle as you go.

Drizzle with the remaining oil and finish with paprika.

Bake, uncovered, for 45 minutes.

The beauty of this is that you can add bigger chunks of cauli and put it over to one side, with more

mac on the other if you have a fussy bunch. Just scoop your favourite section. It's win-win. If you really want to add a third win though, cut the cauli superfine and they won't be able to pick it out.

Inactivewear, TV remote, a Stable Table, do not disturb sign … you know the drill here.

Serves 8

Cauli Corn Mac'n'Cheese

Some foods I seem only able to make in trough-loads. This usually applies to pasta because I love it so much.

Thurs

We are not even typing the full day anymore. What's in the freezer? What's left over? What can we pimp? Is there a one-pan saviour? Do I need to blitz those wilting herbs into a flavour slurry? Are there ANY grown-ups around??

1 head of broccoli,
  florets chopped
1 onion, finely chopped
2 tablespoons olive oil
1 lemon
3 tablespoons chopped chives
½ cup (50 g) finely grated
  parmesan
445 g (15½ oz) good-quality
  shortcrust pastry
4 cups (120 g) loosely packed
  basil leaves
250 g (9 oz) frozen spinach,
  thawed and squeezed

1 cup (25 g) oregano leaves
500 g (1 lb 2 oz) fresh ricotta,
  crumbled
5 eggs, lightly beaten (reserve
  1 teaspoon for the egg wash)
sea salt and freshly ground
  black pepper

OPTIONAL INGREDIENTS
world peace, extra parmesan,
extra lemon zest ... actually
these are ALL essential

LIKE ANYTHING YOU grow up with, you have no idea how good it is until you go forth into the world and learn only by comparison.

I am taking a similar approach with my children.

Except I expect them to deliver unwarranted statements declaring the many reasons I am great.

Mum was right though. And making your own pastry is a calming, meditative ritual, although one that I rarely have time for.

So this recipe pimps something store-bought to make it feel more like homemade.

Preheat the oven to 180°C (350°F).

Saute the broccoli and onion in the oil over medium heat for 10 minutes, then remove from the heat. Grate the zest of the lemon over the broccoli mix as it cools.

Fold and knead the chives and parmesan into the pastry, bring together into a ball then wrap in plastic wrap and set aside to rest.

Blitz the basil, spinach and oregano until fine in a food processor.

Combine the ricotta and beaten egg (except the teaspoon you've remembered to keep back) in a large bowl and fold through the blitzed basil mixture. Season with salt and pepper if you think it needs it.

Roll out the pastry to a 40 cm (16 inch) round about 5 mm (⅛ inch) thick and place on a pizza tray.

Place the broccoli mixture in the middle and top with the herby ricotta, leaving a 7 cm (2¾ inch) pastry band around the edge.

Fold the pastry up and over the filling as much as you can, pinching and pleating it to seal.

Whisk together the reserved egg and 1 tablespoon of water to make an egg wash.

Brush the egg wash over the pastry. Bake for 30–40 minutes, until the edges are golden and the centre is springy to touch.

Serve warm or cold.

Serves 6–8

Broccoli & Cheese Pie

Mum was great at pastry. She used to tell me, 'Loody, you should pay attention; I am great at pastry.'

6 chicken thigh fillets
½ cup (75 g) plain
 (all-purpose) flour
1½ teaspoons onion powder
1 tablespoon chicken
 stock powder
3 eggs
2½ cups (150 g) panko
 breadcrumbs
1 tablespoon dried rosemary
1 kg (2 lb 3 oz) potatoes, peeled
 and cut into rough 5 cm
 (2 inch) angular chunks,
 resembling shards

1 cup (250 ml) chicken stock
½ cup (125 ml) white wine
juice of 1 lemon
1 teaspoon sweet paprika
sea salt
rice bran oil, for shallow-frying
1 baby cos lettuce, cut into
 wedges and washed
vinai-no-regrette (see page 194),
 for dressing

OPTIONAL INGREDIENTS
sauerkraut, aioli and lemon
wedges

THESE ARE THE ORIGINAL form of a chip; the pointy chunks would be chipped from each potato with a little knife.

But more importantly, the shape of these chips allows for tangy chewy down one end and crispy delicious down another.

This combo of the BEST cut of chook, fried crispy things, heaps of umami goodness and a tangy punch to go with it is my idea of heaven.

You can also make the schnitz as far as crumbing, then freeze and fry on demand. It's a laborious procedure so you may as well treat your future self like a queen and do some for her.

Kitchen bashers are wonderful when you need them, and spend the rest of their time arguing their importance with other utensils. I like to use a wooden weighty thing for this (traditional rolling pin, or a favourite my dad made from an old chair leg) rather than a metal mallet.

Preheat the oven to 200°C (400°F).

Place each chicken thigh between two pieces of baking paper and smack it out firmly to 1.5 cm (½ inch) thick. Don't be too rough or you end up with sections breaking up. A thigh schnitzel does result in a wonderfully misshaped crown affair – all the more spots for the crumb.

Combine the flour, onion powder and stock powder in one bowl.

Crack the eggs into another bowl and lightly beat.

Mix together the panko crumbs and dried rosemary in a third bowl.

Then line a baking tray for the finished schnitz.

Dust the chicken pieces in flour, drench in egg and press into the crumbs, then place on the tray.

Repeat this until your fingers are bulbous with crumb – E.T. fingers are a suitable gauge. Rinse and continue until finished. (Or use skewers to avoid this situation.)

Set aside until ready to fry.

Toss the potato shards in the stock, wine, lemon juice, paprika and salt to taste, then tip into a roasting tin and spread them out. Roast for 40 minutes, flipping halfway through.

Heat about 5 mm (¼ inch) of rice bran oil in a non-stick frying pan over medium heat and cook the schnitzels for about 3 minutes each side.

You want them golden and cooked through. It's best to fry in batches to achieve this.

This close to the end of the week you would hope the salad has at least attempted to make itself, and to be fair … it kinda has. Leaves + dressing.

Eat with the schnitties and shards.

Serves 4

Chicken Schnitty & Chips

This dinner is so loved at our house
I use it to manipulate everyone.

⅓ cup (90 g) red curry paste
(to make a zero chilli option,
head to page 200)
200 ml (7 fl oz) coconut cream
1 x 1.3 kg (2 lb 14 oz) chicken,
spine removed, flattened*
2 cups (400 g) jasmine rice
1 stick lemongrass, cut into
3 cm lengths
3 makrut lime leaves, torn
2 tablespoons vegetable oil
1 leek, white and pale green part
only, sliced into 1 cm (½ inch)
thick rounds

250 g (9 oz) cherry tomatoes,
halved
1 bunch baby bok choy,
cut into 2 cm (¾ inch) pieces
1 tablespoon chicken
stock powder

SIDE SALAD
1 teaspoon sesame oil
2 teaspoons lime juice
1 teaspoon brown sugar
1 teaspoon fish sauce
handful of Thai basil leaves

2–3 spring onions (scallions),
white and green parts
sliced on an angle
handful of bean sprouts, trimmed

OPTIONAL INGREDIENTS
lime cheeks

I REMEMBER WHEN I first made this and wondered was I going a bit too far with the whole 'one pan' thing.

Halfway through the process of placing a raw chicken on a bed of watery uncooked rice, the same instinct that repels me from licking something off a bus seat or picking up after my dog barehanded urgently sent alarm neurons to check that I wasn't completely high.

I wasn't, but didn't immediately dismiss the alert.

I resigned myself to the fact that it probably wouldn't work, and if so we could eat scrambled eggs.

We did not eat scrambled eggs.

Combine the curry paste and coconut cream in a dish large enough to hold the chicken. Add the chook and coat well, then leave to marinate for at least 20 minutes (put it in the fridge if this nudges over half an hour).

Preheat the oven to 180°C (350°F).

Combine the rice, lemongrass, makrut lime leaves, oil, leek, tomatoes, bok choy and chicken stock powder in a bowl.

Oil a medium baking dish and add the rice mixture. Pour in 1 cup (250 ml) of water.

Place the chicken on top of the rice, skin-side up, and drizzle with any remaining marinade. (This is the bit you have to do without thinking about it too much.)

Bake for 1 hour. Usually a flat chook will roast in 45 minutes, but an extra 15 gets us over to the safe side. The rice actually steams up under the chook too.

Remove from the oven and rest for 15 minutes before serving.

To make the salad, mix together the sesame oil, lime juice, brown sugar and fish sauce. Toss with the greens.

---

*I talk about flattening a chook on page 72. It's a great thing to master because it cuts your cooking time and gives you a flat plate of chicken skin to apply flavours to.

Serves 6

Red Curry Chicken with Chewy Rice

Chewy rice. It doesn't sound like it should be the selling point, but it is.

A Very Basic Biryani – of Sorts

My love of rice cooked with big flavours continues.

vegetable oil, for pan-frying
500 g (1 lb 2 oz) lamb mince
½ small red onion, halved
   and thinly sliced
1 teaspoon curry powder
3 cardamom pods,
   lightly bruised
¼ teaspoon ground cinnamon
1 tablespoon curry leaves
3 tablespoons sultanas
   or currants
½ teaspoon mustard seeds

2 tablespoons tomato paste
   (concentrated puree)
200 ml (7 fl oz) coconut milk
1 cup (200 g) basmati rice
2 cups (500 ml) chicken stock
1 tablespoon sea salt
2 handfuls of baby spinach

OPTIONAL INGREDIENTS
pappadums, plain yoghurt, thinly
sliced cucumber and mint leaves

THURSDAY. WHAT DID YOU WORK on this week? A casually loaded question. Usually asked when all you've done is tie up incredibly frayed loose ends.

My favourite reply to this is 'success'.

This is a good one for a Thursday-success-work-in-progress evening because it can be made mainly with your right hand so you can cradle a perfectly matched gin and tonic in the other.

Preheat the oven to 200°C (400°F).

Heat a splash of oil in an ovenproof frying pan over medium–high heat.

I'm now going to share an ingenious little trick with you I learnt a while ago.

Make the mince into a big patty. Place it in the pan and just let it brown … like a burger.

Then flip chunks at a time, let them brown and then keep breaking up those chunks into smaller pieces.

Browning meat can result in over-stirring, thereby reducing the heat in the pan and giving you that charming armpit sweat smell of stewed mince. Hell no.

Add the onion and cook for another 5 minutes, until the mince is cooked through.

Add the curry powder, cardamom, cinnamon, curry leaves, sultanas or currants and mustard seeds and fry for a few minutes until fragrant.

Stir in the tomato paste and coconut milk.

Add the rice and stir to ensure everything is evenly coated.

Pour in the stock and season with salt.

Place in the oven and bake for 20 minutes or until the rice is cooked through.

Eat with fresh spinach leaves.

Serves 4

Meatball Snack Hack x 3

The hors d'oeuvre of the immature. Obviously I'm in.
Make. Freeze. Fry, bake or chuck in a pasta sauce at the drop of a button.

Beef & Broccoli

400 g (14 oz) beef sausages
120 g (4½ oz) broccoli florets,
 blitzed until fine
1½ tablespoons onion relish
rice bran oil, for pan-frying

Squeeze the sausage meat
out of the casings, then mix in
a bowl with the broccoli and
onion relish until well combined.

Wet your hands and roll
teaspoons of the mixture into
small meatballs (you're aiming
for about 36).

Pan-fry in batches in a splash
of oil over medium–high heat
for 3 minutes each side, or until
golden and cooked through.

Uncooked meatballs can be
stored in the freezer, and then
baked from frozen in a 180°C
(350°F) oven for 20 minutes.

Makes about 36 small meatballs

Chicken & Corn

400 g (14 oz) chicken sausages
3 tablespoons drained tinned
 corn kernels
3 tablespoons thinly sliced
 spring onion (scallion)
rice bran oil, for pan-frying

Squeeze the sausage meat
out of the casings, then mix in
a bowl with the corn and spring
onion until well combined.

Wet your hands and roll
teaspoons of the mixture into
small meatballs (you're aiming
for about 36).

Pan-fry in batches in a splash
of oil over medium–high heat
for 3 minutes each side, or until
golden and cooked through.

Uncooked meatballs can be
stored in the freezer, and then
baked from frozen in a 180°C
(350°F) oven for 20 minutes.

Makes about 36 small meatballs

Lamb & Spinach

400 g (14 oz) lamb sausages
½ cup (80 g) chopped
 frozen spinach
1½ tablespoons tomato relish
rice bran oil, for pan-frying

Squeeze the sausage meat
out of the casings, then mix
in a bowl with the spinach
and tomato relish until well
combined.

Wet your hands and roll
teaspoons of the mixture into
small meatballs (you're aiming
for about 36).

Pan-fry in batches in a splash
of oil over medium–high heat
for 3 minutes each side, or until
golden and cooked through.

Uncooked meatballs can be
stored in the freezer, and then
baked from frozen in a 180°C
(350°F) oven for 20 minutes.

Makes about 36 small meatballs

1 head broccoli, cut into florets with long stems
1 tablespoon olive oil
2 scotch fillet steaks, butcher-cut 3 cm (1¼ inch) thick, oiled and salted
50 g (1¾ oz) butter
100 g (3½ oz) field or forest mushrooms, chopped
sea salt and freshly ground black pepper
½ cup (125 ml) red wine

1 cup (250 ml) single (pure) cream

OPTIONAL INGREDIENTS
WINE

THIS HAS ALL THE ELEMENTS for an impressive candle-lit wine-lubricated date night.

But somehow over text, 'date' translated as 'budget' and the whole thing accidentally became a one-pan situation.

So here you go babe.

Steak in a pan.

Pan-fry the broccoli in the oil over medium–high heat for 5 minutes, until beginning to char on the edges. Set aside on a plate.

Pan-fry the steaks for 4 minutes each side for medium–rare. Remove and rest for 4 minutes.

Add the butter and mushroom to the same pan and fry for 2 minutes until golden. Season well with salt and pepper.

Deglaze the pan with the wine for 1 minute, then reduce the heat to medium–low, add the cream and bring to a simmer.

Slice the steak and return to the pan, along with the broccoli. Gently toss to coat in the sauce (you can let the steak simmer for a bit longer here if you prefer it a bit more done).

Whisk straight to the table in the pan and face the impending questions relating to 'personal' and 'business' expenses. (Best answered with eyes that say, 'well, this dinner was supposed to be personal, so ...')

Serves 2

One-pan Steak, Broccoli & Shrooms

Was going to set the table, then the agenda changed.

Salmon with Dill Sauce & Spring Spaghetti

I hope the sun is shining the day you make this.

1 kg (2 lb 3 oz) whole salmon
  fillet, skin on, pin-boned
1 tablespoon olive oil
sea salt
3 zucchini (courgettes), julienned
2 bunches asparagus, julienned
  (or if you don't have the
  patience, halved lengthways,
  or quartered if fat)
250 g (9 oz) angel hair pasta

DILL SAUCE
3 tablespoons grated parmesan
½ cup (125 ml) vinai-no-regrette
  (see page 194)
handful of dill, finely chopped
1 tablespoon olive oil

OPTIONAL INGREDIENTS
dill sprigs, and I feel like chablis
is fitting

ASPARAGUS WILL HAVE JUST changed in price from 1 human soul per bunch to 'buy 1, get 3', and you've worn a floaty number once or twice already as winter* eases.

Preheat the oven to 220°C (425°F) and bring a saucepan of heavily salted water to the boil.

Place the salmon, skin-side down, on a baking tray lined with baking paper. Brush with oil and season with salt. This goes in for a total of 15 minutes (or 20 for more well done). You don't have time for a ciggie or any other disgusting habit while this cooks because you need to do other stuff … it's a super-fast dish, this one.

Place your divinely julienned vegetables in the colander you intend to drain the pasta into.

Add the pasta to the boiling water. I always cook angel hair for 1–2 minutes less than it says on the box. It's thinner than my daughter's snow fluff hair and I'd probably consider steaming it if I could.

Drain the pasta over the veg. Place this beautiful tendrilly mess on a platter to create a nest for the salmon.

Break the salmon into chunks and nestle around the pasta (if you don't like the skin wet you could pan-fry that separately for crisp shards, or I'm pretty sure if you cut eye, nose and mouth holes into it it'd be better than most peel-off face masks).

For the sauce, blitz all the ingredients in a small blender. Drizzle generously over the salmon and spaghetti.

---

*This little mojo uplifter is for people living in places that actually *have* a winter. I wore socks to bed once in 2020, and I'm pretty sure it had more to do with laziness than arctic temps.

Serves 4

1 red onion, roughly chopped
1 chorizo, sliced
400 g (14 oz) tin white beans,
  drained* and rinsed
½ bunch kale, stalks removed
  and leaves torn
4 garlic cloves, roughly chopped
½ cup (125 ml) red wine vinegar
2 tablespoons olive oil
250 g (9 oz) short pasta
  (any kind you like)

GREMOLATA
½ cup (50 g) grated parmesan
grated zest of 1 lemon
1 kale leaf, finely shredded
1 teaspoon sea salt

OPTIONAL INGREDIENTS
chilli flakes

THIS SERVES FOUR, but with less pasta because you have the meaty little white beans backing you up. You can go harder on the carbs if you like.

Preheat the oven to 200°C (400°F).

Bring a large saucepan of salted water to the boil.

In a baking dish, massage the onion, chorizo, beans, kale and garlic with the vinegar and oil.

Roast in the oven for 15 minutes.

At the same time, cook the pasta until al dente – I used orecchiette, which takes about 13 minutes.

Drain the pasta, but keep a cup of the water.

Remove the dish from the oven, toss in the hot pasta and mix it all about with a few slurps of the pasta water.

Combine the gremolata ingredients and shower over the dish.

*This step should come with a trigger warning for vegans! Is there an aquafaba food bank out there that I don't know about?

Serves 4

Chorizo
Pan Pasta

I often throw things in the oven so I
have time to remove my bra/make-up/
attitude instead of stirring at the stove.

6 chicken cutlets (thighs),
  skin on, bone in
sea salt and freshly ground
  black pepper
1 onion, roughly chopped
about 8 sprigs lemon thyme,
  leaves stripped
1 head of garlic, halved
  horizontally
10 kipfler potatoes, peeled
  and halved
1 litre (34 fl oz) chicken stock

400 g (14 oz) tin baby lentils,
  drained and rinsed
1 tablespoon dijon mustard
500 g (1 lb 2 oz) green beans,
  trimmed

OPTIONAL INGREDIENTS
light shower of chopped flat-leaf
parsley, lemon wedges

THE FIRST TIME I COOKED this
I'd had one of those mornings
of changing into several outfits
before returning to the first. By
dinner, nothing had changed.

Hmmm, do I roast or braise the
chicken? I want braise, but I want
crispy. Ahhh what to do, what to
do, two pans? But then of course,
full circle, I know how to do it!

Oven cranked (the exact temp for
cranked is 200°C/400°F).

Place a big heavy flameproof
roasting tin over medium–high
heat.

Add the chicken, skin-side down,
and sear for 5 minutes until crispy
and golden. Season, then remove
to a plate.

Lower the heat to medium and
saute the onion and lemon thyme
in the rendered chicken fat for
5 minutes until softened and
fragrant. Add the garlic, cut-side
down, and cook for a further
3 minutes.

Throw in the kipflers. Hands down
the best potato for this type of
thing. So waxy they are almost
exactly like cooled mouldable
wax – I know this because I once
ate a wax jelly bean my dad made
as a practical joke.

Toss these about until the edges
start to go translucent, 3 minutes
or so.

Add the chicken stock, lentils
and dijon, then bake in the oven
for 25 minutes.

Stir the beans through and place
the chicken on top, skin-side up.
Bake for a further 20 minutes.

The skin will be crisp, the
vegetables braised and saucy.

#wontregret

Serves 4

Chicken Braise'n'Bake

File this under #delicious immediately, but then also tag it as #dinnerparty, #longlunch, #midweekeasy.

850 g (1 lb 14 oz) ling or other white fish fillets, skin removed and pin-boned, cut into 5 cm (2 inch) chunks

700 g (1 lb 9 oz) salmon fillet, skin removed and pin-boned, cut into 5 cm (2 inch) chunks

3 tablespoons plain (all-purpose) flour

⅔ cup (160 g) creme fraiche

3 tablespoons dijon mustard

1 tablespoon olive oil, plus extra for drizzling

1 onion, chopped

4 anchovies, chopped

⅓ cup (60 g) capers

4 garlic cloves, finely chopped

200 g (7 oz) baby spinach

1 cup (140 g) frozen peas

⅔ cup (20 g) chopped flat-leaf parsley

1 teaspoon chilli powder, plus extra for the potato (or sweet paprika if you prefer no heat)

1 kg (2 lb 3 oz) potatoes of a similar size

½ cup (120 g) kewpie mayonnaise

lemon wedges, to serve

OPTIONAL INGREDIENTS
nothing – your job here is done, my friend

TO CLARIFY, it's loosely a pie.

It's kind of a salad, potatoes and fish dinner put together with all the condiments and baked.

Preheat the oven to 200°C (400°F).

Combine the ling, salmon, flour, creme fraiche and dijon mustard in a bowl.

Heat the oil in a frying pan over medium heat and saute the onion for 5 minutes.

Add the anchovy, capers and garlic and saute for 5 minutes.

Add the spinach, peas, parsley and chilli powder and saute for 5 minutes.

Set aside to cool slightly.

Meanwhile, boil the potatoes in heavily salted water until soft at the edges.

Drain, then smash the potatoes to break them up.

Toss together the spinach and fish mixtures. Spoon into a 35 cm (14 inch) round baking dish.

Gently combine the smashed potato with the kewpie mayo and extra chilli powder and place on top of the fish mixture.

Drizzle with oil.

Bake in the oven for 25 minutes or until the potato topping is crisp and golden. Serve with lemon wedges.

Serves 6

Tartare
Fish Pie

OK, the 'pie' bit is definitely an upsell,
but honestly it meets the bar set at this
stage of the week, so just enjoy it.

Ham, Cheese & Tomato Tart

The crossroads between a patisserie and the school tuckshop.

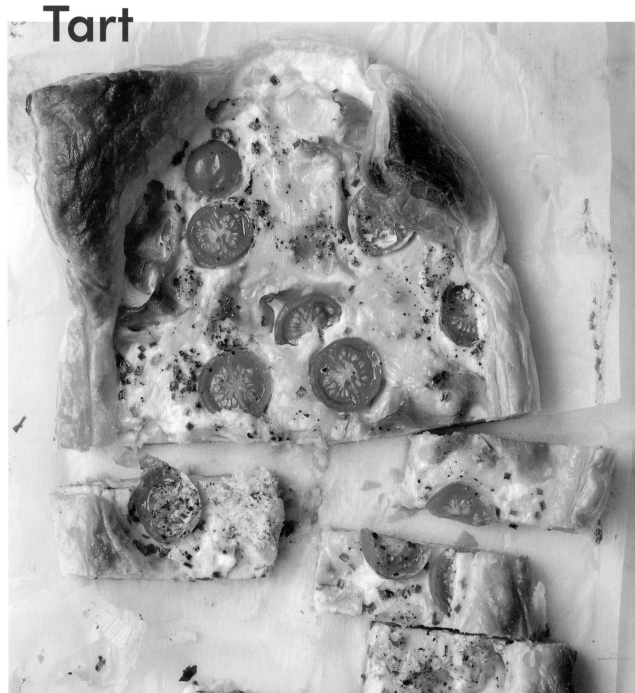

375 g (13 oz) roll good-quality
    puff pastry*, thawed
200 g (7 oz) shaved ham
6 eggs, lightly beaten (set aside
    2 tablespoons for brushing
    the pastry)
¾ cup (185 ml) single (pure)
    cream
1 cup (140 g) finely chopped**
    or grated cheddar
2 tablespoons chopped chives
1 tablespoon sea salt

7 cherry tomatoes, halved

OPTIONAL INGREDIENTS
a sunny day and a soft-floored
destination

THIS WORKS EQUALLY WELL as
an easy dinner, fantastic picnic
food or next-day lunchbox filler.

You can add a salad or some
garlic greens.

I feel the quiche is due for a
comeback. It's hot on the heels
of focaccia and, depending which
year you read this, we might be
revisiting the ol' height = flavour
concept or even devilled eggs.

Like fashion, food gets to return.
It wraps back around after a long
enough interval for the next
generation to think they own it.

TBH I am probably just rewriting
my grandmother's cookbook.

Preheat the oven to 200°C
(400°F).

Place the pastry in a 35 cm x
25 cm (14 inch x 10 inch) baking
dish lined with baking paper.

Poke it a bit with a fork.

Arrange the ham in little clusters
on the pastry.

Whisk together the eggs, cream,
cheddar, chives and salt.

Pour over the ham.

Polka-dot the cherry toms,
cut-side up, on top.

Mix 2 tablespoons of water with
the reserved 2 tablespoons of
egg and brush over the pastry.

Bake for 20 minutes, until the
filling is set and the pastry is
crisp and golden.

---

*I use Careme because they do a rectangu-
lar sheet, but you could just mash together
two squares to suit the pan or dish you'll
be baking in.

**Yes, grating would be a hell of a lot easier,
but my box grater is more often strapped
onto the arms of a child as battle armour
than in my utensil drawer, so chopped it is.
If your grater happens to be in your kitchen,
ready for action, then by all means use it.

Serves 4–6

1 large eggplant (aubergine), cut
    into 1 cm (½ inch) thick slices
⅓ cup (80 ml) olive oil
sea salt and freshly ground
    black pepper
1 teaspoon dried oregano
3 tablespoons pesto
    (see page 206)
200 g (7 oz) fresh ricotta
1 cup (160 g) frozen spinach,
    thawed
1 tablespoon grated lemon zest

1 cup (250 ml) tomato passata
    (pureed tomatoes)
225 g (8 oz) fresh lasagne sheets,
    blanched for 1 minute
2 cups (500 ml) beshy
    (see page 204)
100 g (3½ oz) mozzarella, sliced

OPTIONAL INGREDIENTS
it's personal, so you decide

WHY SHOULD THINGS be shared? Why should they only be made big?

I mean of course this would feed a family, but not in my house because EVERYONE hates eggplant. And quite honestly, I allow them this sentiment because it suits me.

This I make for myself, ready for the next time I need a mental-health day from dinner.

Also, my editor asked if you really need to blanch fresh lasagne sheets? Well. If you want to make it like me, then yes.

I like softer delicate lasagne pies. Not ones that have used all the moisture reserves to quench a sheet of carbs.

But if you don't want to, you don't need to. In the same sentiment, you could also cut down on washing up by throwing fresh spaghetti into a pot of bolognese without additional water.

Totally a personal choice. And my choices are very often irregular and unpredictable.

Preheat the oven to 180°C (350°F).

Spread out the eggplant slices on a large lined baking tray.

Brush with 2 tablespoons of the oil, salt well and sprinkle with oregano.

Roast for 10 minutes. Remove and leave to cool, then drizzle with the pesto.

Mix together the ricotta, spinach, lemon zest, 1 teaspoon of salt and ¼ teaspoon of pepper in a bowl.

In a 35 cm x 20 cm/14 inch x 8 inch baking dish, layer like this:

Oil, 1 tablespoon
Passata, 3 tablespoons
Lasagne, to cover
Ricotta mix, half of it
Passata, 3 tablespoons
Lasagne, to cover
Eggplant, all of it
Beshy, half of it
Lasagne, to cover
Passata, 3 tablespoons
Ricotta mix, the rest of it
Lasagne, to cover
Passata, the rest of it
Beshy, the rest of it

Oil, the rest of it
Mozzarella, all of it.

Then bake for 40 minutes or until golden and bubbling.

Serves 4

A Very Personal Lasagne

This is exactly like those great little personal sourdoughs you can buy. Intentionally made for the grazing of an individual.

Friday

Phew. Friday family fun. Why do you feel more relaxed and patient? Because they can 'decorate' their own pizza, DIY san choy bau cups, or just stay on the trampoline until hunger or an elbow in the eye brings them in. It's movie night with custom pimped popcorn for some and wine for others (me).

2 chicken breast fillets (about 500 g/1 lb 2 oz), chopped into 1 cm (½ inch) cubes
4 cups (740 g) leftover cold rice (jasmine, basmati, brown … doesn't matter)
2 eggs, beaten
4 cm (1½ inch) knob of ginger, grated
2 spring onions (scallions), finely chopped
2 tablespoons rice bran oil

1 tablespoon chicken stock powder
1 teaspoon sugar
1 teaspoon sesame oil

MARINADE
2 teaspoons grated ginger
⅓ cup (80 ml) mirin
1 teaspoon sugar
2 tablespoons sesame oil
1 teaspoon sea salt

VEGGIES
1 tablespoon rice bran oil
1 cup (135 g) grated zucchini (courgette)
1 cup (140 g) frozen peas
1 cup (155 g) grated carrot
½ teaspoon sea salt

OPTIONAL INGREDIENTS
chilli

WHEN THERE'S EXTRA kids to feed, fried rice is the best way to deal with the situation because you can clear out the fridge while nourishing the posse.

The formula for this recipe is pretty traditional, without the addition of soy sauce or other assumed ingredients.

The egg is tossed raw through the cold rice, resulting in glossy and crispy separated grains.

You can switch the chicken for prawns or pork, or even mince.

Keep some of the chopped spring onion green bits for sprinkling at the end if you like.

Everyone has to eat this outside because rice on the floor has similar murderous irritation powers to someone chewing a banana in your ear.

Combine the marinade ingredients in a bowl. Add the chicken and turn to coat well, then leave to marinate while you get on with the other ingredients.

For the veggies, heat the oil in a frying pan over medium–high heat. Add the vegetables and salt and cook for a few minutes until softened.

Tip the vegetables onto a plate and put the pan back over medium–high heat.

Add the chicken and cook for 10 minutes until golden and cooked through. Remove from the pan.

Place the rice in a bowl, pour the egg over and gently toss with a fork, breaking up any clumps so that every grain is coated.

Fry the ginger and spring onion in the rice bran oil over high heat for a few minutes until it starts to brown and smells fantastic. Add the eggy rice and stir well.

Add the stock powder and sugar and cook, stirring, for 5 minutes or so until the grains begin to turn golden.

Return the vegetables and chicken to the pan and stir until warmed through. Finish with the sesame oil.

Serves 4–6

Fried Rice

Friday dinners at our house often involve a quick head count to assess how many kids have gathered.

1 tablespoon olive oil
1 kg (2 lb 3 oz) beef mince
1 tablespoon dried oregano
2 teaspoons ground cumin
2 teaspoons smoked paprika
1 teaspoon ground coriander
1 onion, chopped
3 garlic cloves, crushed
1 tablespoon tomato paste
  (concentrated puree)
400 g (14 oz) tin black beans,
  drained and rinsed
400 g (14 oz) tin chopped
  tomatoes
2 tablespoons sea salt

100 g (3½ oz) corn chips
big dollop of sour cream

CHEESE SAUCE
2 cups (500 ml) beshy
  (see page 204)
½ cup (125 ml) milk
2 cups (200 g) grated cheddar
1 cup (125 g) grated mozzarella

GUAC
3 small avocados, roughly
  chopped
juice of 1 lime
1 teaspoon sea salt
1 tablespoon chopped spring
  onion (scallion), green part only

1 tablespoon chopped coriander
  (cilantro)
1 tablespoon chopped pickled
  jalapeno

TOMATO SALSA
2 roma tomatoes, chopped
1 golden shallot, chopped
1 tablespoon olive oil
1 teaspoon red wine vinegar
1 teaspoon sea salt
1 teaspoon sugar

OPTIONAL INGREDIENTS
a margarita, although this could
be classed as essential

'YO, WHAT DO YOU FEEL LIKE FOR DIN ...'

'NACHOS!'

Fair call. I mean, does anyone order the nachos any more when eating out?

There are so many variables and so many things that could go wrong.

This is definitely a 'do try this at home' dish.

How we like it:

Black beans added to the meat.

Avos make the kids hurl so the guac gets to be spicy, super limey and up our end of the table.

Chips point up so every single one is soggy AND crispy.

And finally ... quite possibly the most important bit ... the cheese is a souped-up bechamel – saucy, stretchy and delicious.

Preheat the oven to 180°C (350°F).

Heat the oil in a large frying pan over high heat and brown the

mince for 5 minutes or so, breaking up any large lumps as you go.

Add the spices, onion and garlic and cook for another 5 minutes until the onion has softened.

Add the tomato paste, black beans and tinned tomatoes. Half-fill the tomato tin with water and swish it around, then add to the pan. Season with the salt.

Simmer over medium heat for 10 minutes so it reduces a bit.

Meanwhile, for the cheese sauce, make the beshy, adding the milk slowly until the sauce is smooth. Fold in the broken cheese until melted and combined. Just fold it in.

Transfer the mince mixture to an ovenproof dish and nestle the corn chips on top.

Drop spoonfuls of cheese sauce over the meat and corn chips.

Bake for 10 minutes until golden and bubbly.

While that's happening, make the guac by combining all the

ingredients in a bowl (I don't make it too smooth).

Ditto for the tomato salsa.

Eat the nachos with the guac, tomato salsa and sour cream.

Serves 6

Beef & Bean Nachos

This is definitely still being made the 'white' way at our house. But the food is going in.

300 g (10½ oz) cooked dry
   shaved noodles*
400 g (14 oz) choy sum,
   blanched

SPICED PORK
500 g (1 lb 2 oz) pork mince
3 tablespoons rice bran oil
1 tablespoon chilli bean sauce
2 tablespoons hoisin sauce
2 teaspoons Sichuan pepper
4 garlic cloves, crushed
1 tablespoon grated ginger

PEANUT SAUCE
3 cups (750 ml) chicken stock
3 tablespoons white miso paste
½ cup (140 g) peanut butter
3 tablespoons oyster sauce
3 tablespoons sesame oil
1½ tablespoons Chinese
   black vinegar
1½ cups (210 g) roasted peanuts
3 tablespoons hoisin sauce
3 tablespoons soy sauce
6 star anise

CUCUMBER SALAD
1 Lebanese (short) cucumber,
   chopped
2 spring onions (scallions),
   thinly sliced
1 teaspoon sesame oil
1 teaspoon sesame seeds
½ teaspoon sea salt

OPTIONAL INGREDIENTS
removing the chilli is optional,
but would likely cause an uproar
with dan dan purists

VARIATIONS ON THIS DISH
come hard and fast.

Naturally I have found a way to
be even more lazy than usual,
involving a pan and the oven,
hence dan dan pan.

Preheat the oven to 220°C (425°F).

For the spiced pork, place all the
ingredients in a large roasting tin
and combine well.

Place in the oven for 20 minutes,
stirring and breaking up any
clumps halfway through.

Meanwhile, put all the peanut
sauce ingredients in a medium
saucepan and bring to a simmer
over medium heat. Cook, stirring,
for 5 minutes until well combined.

Pour the sauce directly over the
pork mince when you remove it
from the oven.

Top with the cooked noodles and
choy sum and toss to combine.

For the cucumber salad, just
bring everything together in
a bowl.

Now you can either serve this
in bowls, or follow our lead and
take great delight in eating from
a trough.

Like drinking from a jar. I'm
surprised this approach hasn't
been explored by hipster cafes.

---

*These are great because they're like frilly
Asian fettuccine and mimic the sauce swirl-
ing ability. But any dry noodle can be used
really – rice, egg or even spaghetti. Just
cook according to the packet instructions.

Serves 4

Dan Dan Pan

More soupy, less meat, richer gravy, sesame-based, greens or not? You can choose your own adventure really.

Pasta à la Bebe

I have been making this blindfolded for about 14 years now.

500 g (1 lb 2 oz) penne
1 tablespoon olive oil
200 g (7 oz) bacon, finely diced
2 cups (270 g) grated zucchini
  (courgette)
185 g (6½ oz) tin tuna in
  olive oil, drained
1 cup (140 g) frozen peas,
  thawed
1 cup (230 g) fresh ricotta

OPTIONAL INGREDIENTS
grated lemon zest and chilli
flakes (for the grown-ups)

THIS HITS YOU STRAIGHT in the boscaiola bone. It's comforting, but breaks the Italian turf vs surf rule, setting you straight back on the edge of rebel where you like to be.

I don't know why I keep coming back to this recipe – there's no onion or garlic or extra salt. It was quite possibly just what I had in the fridge one day when I was a young single mum.

But getting married, learning more about nutrition and having two more kids hasn't changed the blueprint.

Cook the pasta in a saucepan of salted water until al dente.

Drain and keep a cup of pasta water aside.

In that same pan, add the oil and fry the bacon and zucchini over medium–high heat until soft and starting to brown.

Add the tuna and peas and cook for 2 minutes.

Tip the pasta back into the pan, along with the ricotta and a good splash of pasta water, and stir until combined and warmed through.

Serves 18 babies or 4 adults

2 quantities of yoghurt flatty
   dough (see page 212; I didn't
   add yeast to these ones)
160 ml (5½ fl oz) veg slap*
   (see page 210)
olive oil, for drizzling
450 g (1 lb) mozzarella ball,
   sliced or grated
sea salt

PIZZA 1
¼ pineapple, core removed,
   thinly sliced
100 g (3½ oz) shaved ham

PIZZA 2
1 zucchini (courgette), cut into
   ribbons with a peeler
½ teaspoon chilli flakes
2 tablespoons chopped oregano

PIZZA 3
1 Italian pork and fennel sausage,
   skin removed, cut into 1 cm
   (½ inch) thick rounds (this
   goes on raw!)
1 grilled artichoke heart,
   cut into 6 pieces
1 grilled capsicum (pepper),
   thinly sliced
handful of rocket (arugula) leaves

PIZZA 4
You know there's always
someone who just wants
a Margie.

OPTIONAL INGREDIENTS
stracciatella cheese (this is just
the inside of a burrata, delight-
ful!), freshly grated parmesan
and/or bocconcini

THE BEAUTY OF THIS IS DIY
chaos and messy fingers. Plus:
they make it, they will generally
eat it … This is the greatest
psychological trick I can share
with you. We all set out to do the
right thing but as soon as you
have more kids than adults in the
house, tactics are implemented.

We try not to use methods that
are too manipulative, but in the
same way you occasionally shock
yourself in a positive way, you can
be equally surprised about your
own bad behaviour. Surprised
AND a little impressed. Trust me.

Preheat the oven to 240°C (475°F).

Divide the dough into four pieces
and roll out into pizza bases.
I like to pull and stretch mine
and make them a bit misshapen.

Lay them out on oiled trays. If you
don't have four trays, people will
just have to wait, possibly even
talk to one another.

Drop 2 tablespoons veg slap
(or tomatoey equivalent) on each
base, followed by a quarter of
the cheese.

Common mistake is cheese
last. Nope, goes on UNDER the
toppings (hence their name!).

Layer your pizzas with stuff –
don't be crazy, less is more.

Drizzle with oil, season with
salt and hit them with your
mediocre domestic oven heat
until bubbling and crisp, about
20 minutes each batch.

You will likely burn at least one,
only a bit and by accident, but
that's what makes life special.

It's exactly like having kids.

---

*If you don't have any slap, crack a 400 g
(14 oz) tin of crushed tomatoes and mix in
1 crushed garlic clove, 1 teaspoon of sea
salt and 2 tablespoons of olive oil. This
makes a quick and easy (possibly drinkable)
slurry to work with.

*Serves 6–8, depending on the age
and size of the consumers
(Makes 4 large pizzas)*

Pizza Night

Pineapple does work on pizza.
Don't @ me.

CHICKEN & CORN

1 kg (2 lb 3 oz) chicken mince
300 g (10½ oz) tin creamed corn
1 tablespoon cornflour
  (cornstarch)
1 egg
1 tablespoon grated ginger
2 spring onions (scallions),
  finely chopped
1 tablespoon sesame oil
1 tablespoon soy sauce
100 wonton wrappers

PORK & PRAWN

1 kg (2 lb 3 oz) pork mince
250 g (9 oz) thawed frozen
  prawn meat, chunky chopped
225 g (8 oz) water chestnuts,
  chopped
1 egg
1 tablespoon cornflour
  (cornstarch)
½ cup (150 g) pickled Asian
  veg*, chopped
2 tablespoons finely chopped
  coriander (cilantro) stem

1 tablespoon soy sauce
2 tablespoons oyster sauce
2 spring onions (scallions),
  finely chopped
1 tablespoon sesame oil
100 wonton wrappers

OPTIONAL INGREDIENTS

any dipping sauce**, and
chicken stock with spring onions
(scallions) and chilli as a broth

IT'S ALWAYS WISE to make a single dumpling and boil it before making the whole lot in case you need to add more flavour. Imagine finishing all 200 and realising they sucked.

Poor kids.

Place all the ingredients for each flavour in separate large bowls and mix until well combined.

Use a teaspoon to make a small mound of filling in the middle of each wonton wrapper.

Wet the edges and fold in half, then squeeze out the excess air and pinch the edges closed.

You can do fancy folds, but until your staff of minors are deft enough with their digits, I would keep it simple.

To cook, you can either steam them over boiling water for 15 minutes, simmer in chicken stock for 10 minutes or, to do a potsticker: place about eight

dumplings in a single layer in an oiled frying pan, add 1 cup (250 ml) of water, and cover. Let this simmer until the water has been absorbed and the bases begin to crisp up – about 15 minutes.

If you're cooking from frozen, add 5 minutes to each step.

_____

*Pickled Asian veg = radish or mustard greens

**You can serve these with pretty much any dipping sauce, but more often than not I throw together my famous dumpling dipping biz (1 tablespoon soy sauce, 1 tablespoon Chinese black vinegar and 1 teaspoon sesame oil). Takes less than 30 seconds. Tastes amazing.

Makes about 200 dumplings all up, but freeze half of each mix for another Friday

Dumplings

This is the perfect Friday night of hunger games in our house. You can eat as many as you can make.

Chicken Breast Nuggets

If you can use a knife unsupervised in the kitchen, you can make these.

2 chicken breast fillets, sliced
   into 1 cm (½ inch) thick strips
½ cup (120 g) kewpie
   mayonnaise
1¼ cups (75 g) panko
   breadcrumbs
rice bran oil, for pan-frying

OPTIONAL INGREDIENTS
sauce, maybe a lemon wedge

IN A BOWL, mix together the
chicken and mayo.

Toss each nugget in the panko
crumbs to coat and place on
a lined tray until ready to cook*.

Heat a couple of tablespoons of
rice bran oil in a frying pan over
medium–high heat and cook the
nugs for 2–3 minutes each side
until golden and cooked through.
Alternatively, preheat the oven to
200°C (400°F), brush or spray with
oil and bake for 10 minutes until
cooked through.

Add a chopped salad and you
and the kids are halfway to
story time.

---

*You can freeze them like this and just
pan-fry from frozen too!

Serves 4 kids

1 onion, chopped or grated
2 carrots, chopped or grated
2 heads of bok choy,
  finely chopped
1 small head of broccoli,
  finely chopped
handful of green beans,
  finely chopped
1 tablespoon olive oil
500 g (1 lb 2 oz) pork mince
5 cm (2 inch) knob of ginger,
  peeled and grated
3 garlic cloves, finely chopped

4 spring onions (scallions),
  chopped
1 teaspoon mirin
3 tablespoons hoisin sauce
3 teaspoons soy sauce
1 tablespoon sesame oil
100 g (3½ oz) vermicelli noodles,
  soaked in boiling water,
  drained and snipped with
  scissors into 2 cm (¾ inch)
  lengths
iceberg lettuce cups or frozen
  pancakes*, to serve

OPTIONAL INGREDIENTS
oyster sauce, fried noodles and
more chopped spring onion
(scallion)

GUYS. IT'S THE END of the week, we're all likely to have a floppy carrot hanging about, maybe you discovered a bag of bok choy you had grand plans for, straggly beans, half a brocc head?

This is the sir-mix-a-lot of wonder. You can add bamboo shoots, water chestnuts, peanuts. Form your own band here. You pretty much can't go wrong at all. You're just looking for about 5 cups of chopped veg in total.

Saute all the chopped vegetables in the oil until tender, then set aside in a big serving bowl.

Saute the pork mince with the ginger, garlic and spring onion until golden.

Add the mirin, hoisin, soy and sesame oil and toss to coat well.

Put the pork mixture and noodles into the bowl with the veg and mix well.

You can eat this with cutlery, but it's infinitely more fun to scoop it into edible vessels like lettuce and pancakes to munch immediately.

---

*Available in the freezer section of Asian supermarkets.

Serves 6

Fridge Giver San Choy Bau

You eat this with your hands which, I can proudly say, my team of heathens is all about.

2 kg (4 lb 6 oz) chicken wings
1 tablespoon curry powder
2 teaspoons smoked paprika
1 teaspoon sea salt
200 g (7 oz) shredded coconut
200 g (7 oz) panko breadcrumbs*

MARINADE

1 kg (2 lb 3 oz) coconut yoghurt
1 tablespoon finely grated
  turmeric**
1 teaspoon sweet paprika
3 teaspoons grated ginger**

2 cloves garlic, crushed**
2 teaspoons onion powder
1 teaspoon ground coriander

OPTIONAL INGREDIENTS

1 chopped green chilli, lime cheeks, coriander (cilantro) leaves, kewpie mayonnaise and/or sriracha

DEEP FROM THE BASEMENT of my brain, all the ingredients and ideas for this dish peered out from behind their hiding spot with squinting eyes and ventured into the open.

They found each other. They began talking. They realised they had power in numbers and then they just stormed my frontal lobe.

It may have even woken me up.

It's now one of the few things I don't try to better or ad lib as a cook.

It works. And it's insanely delicious.

Combine the marinade ingredients in a large container with a lid. Add the wings and massage until each one is well coated***. Cover and put them in the fridge.

Try to do this yesterday, or at least this morning, or at the very least, an hour before you want to cook them. The longer the better.

When you are ready to cook, preheat the oven to 180°C (350°F).

Take the wings out of the fridge and bring to room temp.

In a large bowl, combine the curry powder, paprika, salt, shredded coconut and panko.

Dip each wing in the crumb mixture so it's well coated and place them on a large baking tray lined with baking paper. Try to give them a little bit of room on the tray so they brown evenly.

Bake for 40 minutes, flipping over once.

*If you can't find panko without palm oil and really don't wish to be involved in that crime, you can use regular dried bread-crumbs massaged with 2 tablespoons of rice bran oil.

**You can sub these for powdered/dried if you like. I get some fresh stuff in when I can but it won't completely ruin the recipe if you don't.

***I use my dishwashing gloves (that I never seem to use for washing dishes) to really get my hands in there. Just rinse and chuck them in the wash afterwards or rely on washing the dishes to clean them. You don't necessarily need them; it's just that the turmeric can stain and leave your mitts looking a little Trump-esque.

Serves 6

Coconut Chilli Wings

This is one of those recipes that just created itself.

3 tablespoons mirin

1 tablespoon soy sauce

½ teaspoon sea salt

1 teaspoon five spice powder

2 duck breasts, skin scored
in hatches

24-pack frozen pancakes*

3 tablespoons hoisin sauce

1 Lebanese (short) cucumber,
sliced diagonally into batons

¼ bunch coriander (cilantro)
sprigs, trimmed, stems
kept long

1 spring onion (scallion), green
part sliced into sticks

OPTIONAL INGREDIENTS

Nope. I mean, you *could* switch
out the pancakes for lettuce
leaves, but that book, my friends,
is hopefully in a different aisle.

ME ON FRIDAY and can't be
bothered: Who wants Chinese
takeaway?

Them: Yes please! Can we get
duck pancakes, a suckling pig,
salt and pepper molluscs and
a garlic lobster?

F*CK!

What I meant: KIDS! YOU'RE
GETTING FRIED RICE AND
PRAWN CRACKERS FOR DINNER.

So now we make this. And
without the delivery fee and the
other excessive options it works
out way cheaper.

Combine the mirin, soy, salt and
five spice in a bowl and use to
coat the duck breasts. Marinate
them in the fridge for as long as
you can – overnight is a great
idea, but an hour is fine.

Bring the duck to room temp
before you cook it.

Place the duck, skin-side down,
in a cold frying pan over low heat
for 10 minutes. The marinade
can burn so check it occasionally,
although a slight char will not
destroy this dish!

Flip the duck over and cook for
5 minutes, then remove the pan
from the heat and rest for another
5 minutes.

Slice the duck thinly and toss
in the pan juices.

Steam or microwave the
pancakes, following the
instructions on the packet.

Let everyone DIY but be
overbearing and make them
do this:

Pancake > hoisin > duck >
cucumber > coriander > spring
onion.

Wrap it > eat it > smile.

---

*Available in the freezer section of Asian
supermarkets.

Serves 4

Duck
Pancakes

You can avoid cooking altogether for these if you have a chop shop nearby. This is for those who don't.

1 cup (125 g) cornflour
  (cornstarch)
1 teaspoon five spice powder
1 teaspoon sea salt
½ teaspoon ground coriander
800 g (1 lb 12 oz) ling fillets, skin
  and bones removed, cut into
  approx. 8 cm x 4 cm (3¼ inch x
  1½ inch) pieces (I like to cut on
  the diagonal, creating shards)
2 cups (500 ml) rice bran oil,
  approx.

2 tablespoons oyster sauce
1 tablespoon hot water
1 teaspoon sesame oil
1 bunch gai lan (or any Asian
  greens), blanched
1 bird's eye chilli, finely chopped
  (remove seeds for less heat)
3 tablespoons coriander
  (cilantro) leaves
3 tablespoons sliced spring onion
  (scallion), green part only

SEASONING MIX
½ teaspoon five spice powder
2 tablespoons sea salt
  or to taste
½ teaspoon freshly ground
  black pepper
½ teaspoon chilli flakes

OPTIONAL INGREDIENTS
steamed rice*, dipping biz (see
tip, page 130), lemon cheeks and
Salt'N'Pepa Spotify playlist

MY AVERSION TO deepish-frying is obvious. It's boring, temperamental and makes your wardrobe smell before you remember to close the door to the hallway.

The fish bit – well, there isn't really an excuse here, except that, unlike other meats, I feel that its purchase must be recipe and time specific. Which I rarely have the patience for when it comes to grocery hunt-and-gather day.

I often promise to collect seafood during the week and then on Thursday become infuriated that there are no reserves and seconds before anger erupts, I realise it's my fault and commit to rectifying the faux pas the next day, inevitably Friday.

Preheat the oven to 150°C (300°F).

Combine the cornflour, five spice, salt and ground coriander in a large bowl.

Toss the ling in the seasoned flour to coat and shake off the excess before frying.

Heat the rice bran oil in a deep non-stick frying pan over high heat. Depending on the size of your pan you may need a little more or less oil, but basically it should be 1 cm (½ inch) deep. It also may require topping up as you fry.

Pan-fry the fish in batches for 30 seconds each side. Place on a baking tray lined with baking paper and keep warm in the oven.

Combine the seasoning mix ingredients and sprinkle it over the fish as it comes out hot from the pan, then add more as necessary to serve or just offer it on the side for peeps to DIY.

Mix the oyster sauce with the hot water and sesame oil and toss with the hot blanched gai lan.

Sprinkle the chilli, coriander and spring onion over the fish and serve hot with the greens.

---

*This just pops in here in the optional section because we are at that stage where you: know how to cook beautiful steamed rice on the stove top, have a rice cooker, are going to read my recipe on page 198, buy an extra container for the freezer when you get takeaway, or get the microwave packs from the shops. Whatever it is, you're on your own for this one. It's Friday.

Serves 4

Salt'n'Pepper Ling

The two things I don't do that often at home are deepish-fry and fish.

TV Snacks x 3

All of these are trumpety versions of old-school classics.

I always chose the strawberry topping as a kid, so this ice-cream sundae
is the fancier adult version.

My first taste of Vegemite and Tabasco with butter was like a slap in the face
… why am I not having this on toast daily? It's the best.

The crack recipe is a combo of stuff from my sisters-in-law – the Jewish
matzoh base from the one married to my brother, and the ginger
in the caramel from my husband's two sisters in NZ.
The miso just seemed right. It is.

Vegemite & Tabasco Popcorn

3 tablespoons popping corn
50 g (1¾ oz) butter
1 teaspoon Vegemite
½ teaspoon Tabasco sauce

Put the popping corn in a brown sandwich bag and microwave on high for about 1 minute, until there are pauses between popping noises.

Combine the butter, Vegemite and Tabasco in a small bowl and melt in the microwave.

Drizzle over the popcorn and toss to coat.

Makes about 3 cups

Miso Crack

230 g (8 oz) unsalted butter
1 tablespoon white miso paste
1 cup (185 g) brown sugar
2 teaspoons ground ginger
3–4 matzoh sheets
200 g (7 oz) chocolate chips

Preheat the oven to 190°C (375°F).

Simmer the butter, miso, brown sugar and ginger for 3 minutes or until well combined and the sugar has dissolved.

Arrange the matzoh in a single layer on a foil-lined baking tray and pour the miso mixture over the top.

Bake for 10 minutes.

Remove from the oven and sprinkle with the chocolate chips while hot. Leave to melt for 5 minutes, then spread evenly.

Set in the fridge for 20 minutes, then crack into pieces when you're ready to eat.

Serves 6–8

Strawberries & Ice Cream

250 g (9 oz) strawberries, hulled and roughly chopped
⅓ cup (75 g) caster (superfine) sugar
1 teaspoon balsamic vinegar
vanilla ice cream
fistful of chopped peanuts

Toss together the strawberries, sugar and balsamic, and leave to macerate for 30 minutes.

Eat with ice cream and nuts.

Serves 4

Saturday

Saturday is the flex day, time to stretch out the repertoire, make gnocchi, braise a ragu, do some yoga, ask a few friends round to eat and make a fancy cocktail or spritz.

1 sourdough loaf
2 cups (500 ml) milk
1 kg (2 lb 3 oz) mixed pork
   and veal mince
1 white onion, diced
3 garlic cloves, crushed
handful of chopped
   flat-leaf parsley
3 tablespoons finely
   chopped oregano
1 tablespoon freshly ground
   black pepper

2 tablespoons sea salt
200 g (7 oz) mozzarella
olive oil spray
½ bunch basil, leaves picked
   and chopped
700 g (1 lb 9 oz) tomato passata
   (pureed tomatoes)

OPTIONAL INGREDIENTS
friends

DEPENDING ON THE time of day, you can enjoy these with reckless abandon.

The joy of eating these, especially with a group of like-minded freaks, will have you sliding into a state of lip-smacking euphoria.

Cut the loaf of sourdough in half. Remove the crust and tear up the bread from one half (about 2 cups worth), and save the other half to serve.

Soak the torn bread in the milk for 20 minutes, then drain and discard the milk.

Place the milky bread, mince, onion, 2 cloves of garlic, parsley, oregano, pepper and salt in a large bowl and mix to combine.

Roll the mixture into eight balls.

Cut the mozzarella into eight 3 cm (1¼ inch) chunks (thinly slice whatever is left and use it to top the meatballs later). Push a chunk of mozza into the centre of each ball, moulding the mince back around it into a ball.

Preheat the oven to 200°C (400°F).

Spray the base of a 35 cm (14 inch) non-stick ovenproof frying pan with oil, then sear the meatballs over high heat for 1–2 minutes each side.

This is a delicate procedure, and you could cheat a bit and just brown them under the grill for 5 minutes a side.

Either way, you are bound to have one that splits but this a super rustic messy affair so embrace whatever happens.

Remove the meatballs from the pan, then place the pan over medium heat. Saute the remaining garlic for 5 minutes, then add the basil, passata and 1½ cups (375 ml) of water and simmer for 5 minutes.

Pop the big boys back in (any splits should face up), and top with the thin slices of mozza.

Bake in the oven for 20 minutes, until cooked through and oozing melted insanity.

No plates + giant chunks of hand-torn bread + linen napkins

+ sauce so red you-better-be-tight = big fat smiles* of 'Really? We're just going in like this?' from your guests.

---

*I will often ignore/wilfully misread a grimace as a smile. I recommend it.

Makes 8

Big Meatballs

These are the biggest, juiciest balls
you will ever manhandle.

1.5 kg (3 lb 5 oz) pork neck
16 tacos

MARINADE
1 cup (250 ml) pineapple juice
1 cup (250 ml) barbecue sauce
3 tablespoons American mustard
1 onion, skin removed and
  quartered
2 teaspoons coriander seeds
1 tablespoon cumin seeds
2 tablespoons dried oregano
1 cinnamon stick

1 head of garlic, cloves peeled
  and lightly crushed
1 tablespoon sea salt

PICKLED PINEAPPLE
2 cups (500 ml) white vinegar
¾ cup (165 g) sugar
1½ tablespoons sea salt
3 cardamom pods, bruised
1 whole pineapple, peeled,
  cored if liked and thinly sliced

SLAW
3 cups (225 g) shredded cabbage
2 tablespoons kewpie
  mayonnaise
juice of 1 lime
2 tablespoons chopped chives
1 teaspoon sea salt

OPTIONAL INGREDIENTS
thinly sliced red onion, coriander
(cilantro) leaves and lime wedges

LOW AND SLOW PORK … all in the pot, lid on, set and forget. No browning.

Pineapple is sweetly pickled with some spices.

If you pre-shred the cabbage, pick the herbs, chop some chives and pack some soft tacos, you've got one killer bring-a-plate set-up that will muscle over anyone else's contribution.

I even took this stable of ponies camping!

Preheat the oven to 120°C (235°F).

Combine all the marinade ingredients in a heavy ovenproof dish with a lid. (I use a Dutch oven; you could also use a slow cooker, but I'm not really sure of the settings.)

Add the pork and turn to coat on all sides.

Place a piece of baking paper over the pork and press it down into the juices – this is like a face mask, keeping the whole thing moist while it cooks. Pop the lid on, place in the oven and cook gently for 6 hours.

Remove and allow to cool, then shred the meat with tongs and stir with all the juices, breaking up the garlic and onion as you go. You can discard harder spices, like the cinnamon stick.

The pork can be made ahead of time, and preheated to serve. You can do this in small batches in the microwave, checking and stirring often, or in a saucepan over medium–low heat, stirring occasionally.

For the pickled pineapple, combine the vinegar, sugar, salt, cardamom and 2 cups (500 ml) of water in a saucepan. Bring to a simmer, then allow to cool slightly.

Place the pineapple in a large airtight jar and pour the pickling liquid over the top. Seal and allow to pickle for at least an hour. Store in the fridge for up to 2 weeks.

To make the slaw, toss all the ingredients together in a bowl.

Warm the taco shells*.

Take all the components to the table and let everyone help themselves.

*A bit of a tip: I really don't like the hard shells you can buy off the shelf – they taste like stale corn chips to me. I choose the soft ones, give them a quick spray with oil and heat in the pan, then let them cool flopped over an old paper towel roll. DIY crispy tacos. Or just keep them soft.

Serves 8

Pulled Pork Tacos with Pickled Pineapple

This is a slippery slide into a heavenly situation. Smoky, delicious and stringy.

olive oil, to coat
sea salt and freshly ground
   black pepper
1 x 1.2 kg (2 lb 10 oz)
   T-bone steak*
850 g (1 lb 14 oz) small
   potatoes, halved
1 head of garlic, top trimmed
   horizontally
2 tablespoons rice bran oil

BEARNIE SAUCE
3 tablespoons white wine vinegar
1 tablespoon dried tarragon
1 golden shallot, chopped
sea salt and freshly ground
   black pepper
2 egg yolks
400 g (14 oz) butter, melted
   and kept warm

OPTIONAL INGREDIENTS
something salady if you gotta

THE FUSS IN THIS ONE is all about cooking the steak, for which *ALERT* you will need a probe thermometer.

The max relax is in the bearnie sauce, which is not made traditionally. It's quite possibly the wrong consistency, but against all odds, it's the slinky minx this piece of beef has been searching for its entire life.

Preheat the oven to 130°C (250°F). Line a baking tray with baking paper.

Oil and salt the meat on both sides, and place on the prepared baking tray. Roast for 45–60 minutes, until the internal temperature reaches 55°C (130°F).

Remove and rest for 15 minutes. Once cool, wrap until you're ready to grill. You can do this a day ahead and store the wrapped meat in the fridge – just make sure you bring it back to room temperature before searing.

When you're ready to start cooking the spuds, preheat the oven to 200°C (400°F).

Boil the potatoes and garlic head in heavily salted water for 15 minutes, or until just tender.

Drain and set the garlic aside. Tip the spuds back in the pan and toss with the rice bran oil. Put the lid on and give them a hard shake to rough up the edges.

Spread out the potatoes on a non-stick baking tray. Lightly oil the garlic head and sit it in the middle, then season everything with salt and pepper.

Roast for 40 minutes or so until golden and crisp.

Meanwhile, for the sauce, combine the vinegar, tarragon, shallot, a big pinch of salt and a decent grinding of pepper in a small saucepan and simmer over medium heat for 5 minutes. Strain to remove the solids and allow to cool slightly.

Place the cooled vinegar, egg yolks and butter in a powerful blender and process on high until smooth and combined (or use a good stick blender, just not a small food processor). The speed

of the blender will emulsify the ingredients while still warm.

As the sauce cools it will firm up a little.

Sear the steak on a very hot chargrill pan or barbecue grill plate for about 5 minutes each side until the outside has reached the desired crispness. The inside will be medium–rare.

As the meat has already rested, you can serve immediately with everything else!

---

*You'll probably have to engage your butcher for this and have it cut to order. I like to go about 5 cm (2 inches) thick. It's a statement steak.

Serves 4

Steak, Bearnie & Golden Spuds

It's Saturday, and if you're this far in you will know two things about me: I'm fancy AND I'm lazy.

1.5 kg (3 lb 5 oz) lamb shoulder,
  bone in
1 tablespoon olive oil
1 carrot, cut into 1 cm
  (½ inch) cubes
1 onion, cut into 1 cm
  (½ inch) cubes
1 celery stick, cut into 1 cm
  (½ inch) cubes
1 teaspoon sea salt
6 garlic cloves, smashed
2 cups (500 ml) white wine

400 g (14 oz) tin crushed
  tomatoes
1 small bunch rosemary
250 g (9 oz) cherry tomatoes
250 g (9 oz) risoni
gremolata (see page 215)

OPTIONAL INGREDIENTS
wine
not optional: napkins

APPARENTLY BEING a good cook doesn't necessarily make you a good host. But replacing the lamb with two large eggplants, quartered, and a couple of big knobs of butter, then reducing the liquid by about half, does, at least where a vegetarian is concerned.

And as an added bonus for not completing your sommeliers course, this dish goes with all the colours of wine.

Preheat the oven to 180°C (350°F).

Put the lamb in a cold Dutch oven or flameproof casserole dish, fat-side down, and brown over medium–high heat for 10 minutes, or until golden on all sides. Remove the lamb and set aside.

Wipe out any burnt bits from the dish, then add the oil and saute the carrot, onion, celery and salt over medium heat for 3 minutes, until softened.

Add the garlic and saute for a further 2 minutes.

Increase the heat to high and deglaze the pan with half the wine.

After 1 minute, add the rest of the wine and the crushed tomatoes. Fill the tomato tin with water and add to the pan too.

Bring to a simmer.

Add the rosemary sprigs and place the lamb on top. Scatter the cherry tomatoes on and around the lamb.

Cover with a cartouche (a piece of baking paper cut to fit the pan) and a tight-fitting lid. Place in the oven for 4½ hours.

Shortly before the lamb is ready, cook the risoni according to the packet instructions.

This is best served in a large open bowl.

Put the risoni in first, then top with the lamb and as much soupy sauce as you like. Finish with a good sprinkling of gremolata.

Invite your guests to shred into the meat with forks, marvelling at the tenderness.

Serves 4

Soupy Greek Lamb Shoulder

I once got so excited about making this that I forgot I'd invited a few vegetarians to lunch.

Cauliflower Gnocchi

OK guys, don't freak out, but it's VEGAN cauliflower gnocchi! I KNOW!

1 head of cauliflower,
    cut into baby florets
1¾ cups (260 g) plain
    (all-purpose) flour
1 tablespoon olive oil*
1 tablespoon sea salt
50 g (1¾ oz) butter
4 sprigs thyme
baby fist of grated parmesan

OPTIONAL INGREDIENTS
I'm going to say plates because
it's almost impossible not to eat
this straight from the pan

(IGNORE THE BUBBLING butter
and crispy parmesan all over it.
The GNOCCHI is vegan.)

This is the ideal weekend project
with kids. It's a messy mashy
affair. Basically playdough, but
generally a more acceptable
version to consume.

Here's the to-do list:

Steam the cauliflower until
tender.

Cool, then squeeze out the
excess water. (I rolled mine in a
fresh tea towel like a sausage,
went and stood in the shower
over the drain, held one end
down with my foot and twisted
the other with my hand. Sure, an
excessive move, but it works. Also
great for quick drying cozzies!)

Finely blitz the cauliflower.

Add the flour and oil.

Blitz again.

Don't worry if you think it's too
gluey. Knead it for a few minutes
and you'll see it isn't.

Roll into long lengths and cut
into pointy slugs.

Drop them into salted boiling
water and scoop them out as
soon as they float to the top.

Now perform some bubbling
magic with them.

Heat the butter, thyme and parmy
in a frying pan over high heat.
As soon as it's bubbling, add
the gnocchi, reduce the heat to
medium and let it get crispy and
delicious underneath.

Wait until crunchy.

F*CKING DELICIOUS ... plus in
spite of being all white it's mainly
vegetable, pretty much vegan
and can be filed under VERY
F*CKING EASY.

---

*Or use garlic parmy oil (see page 192)
for a non-vegan version.

Serves 6

Roast Chicken on Corn Trivet

This might be one of my favourite dishes of all time.

3 corn cobs, husks and silks removed, cut reasonably evenly into 4 cm (1½ inch) pieces
1 bunch thyme
1 x 1.5 kg (3 lb 5 oz) chicken
3 tablespoons olive oil, plus extra for pan-frying
1 teaspoon sea salt
½ teaspoon sweet paprika
1 tablespoon white miso paste
50 g (1¾ oz) butter

1 bunch cavolo nero (Tuscan kale), tough ribs discarded, leaves and tender ribs kept whole

OPTIONAL INGREDIENTS
a bit of lemon zest, but really, just do this one as is

I OWE MY INTRODUCTION to corn and miso to my friend and incredible chef, Danielle Alvarez, the kindest of people, who boldly dared to co-host an Instagram Live cooking session with me during Covid. I managed to turn the whole thing into mild chaos because I cooked over an open wood-fuelled flame (*why*?!) and my logs got cold. The result was still an immaculate marriage.

But that is what I love about food in the first place: there are so many mistakes on the way to so many wonderful discoveries.

Preheat the oven to 200°C (400°F).

Oil a large roasting tin.

Stand the corn cobs up in the tin to create a trivet for the chicken.

Scatter the thyme sprigs over the base.

Massage the chicken with the oil, salt and paprika, and place on the corn cobs.

Pour 1½ cups (375 ml) of water into the base of the tin.

Roast the chicken for 1 hour. Check it's cooked by piercing the thigh meat and making sure the juices run clear.

Drain the juices from the chicken and set aside to rest.

Remove all the thyme sprigs you can from the tin.

Cut the kernels from the corn and return to the tin with the miso, butter and ½ cup (125 ml) of water.

Place over low heat and allow this to bubble and braise for about 15 minutes.

Pan-sear the cavolo nero in a splash of oil in a separate pan. Or simply blanch in boiling water – there's enough flavour to bring this baby to the party if you want to avoid washing up another pan.

Serve succulent slices of chook, with the greens and the sweet sauciness of the miso, butter and corn braise.

Serves 4–6

2 racks pork ribs

MARINADE
1 head of garlic, halved
horizontally
1 tablespoon onion powder
2 teaspoons smoked paprika
2 teaspoons sea salt
2 teaspoons freshly ground
black pepper
2 teaspoons ground cumin
½ cup (125 ml) Worcestershire
sauce

1 cup (250 ml) barbecue sauce
½ cup (100 g) brown sugar
½ cup (125 ml) apple cider
vinegar

FOIL SPUDS
4 large potatoes, poked once
with a fork and wrapped in foil
½ cup (125 g) sour cream
baby fist of chopped chives
sea salt

OPTIONAL INGREDIENTS
butter for the spuds, and a slaw
would work (see page 31)

TO MY HORROR, Mum once absent-mindedly collected the discarded chicken wings off my boyfriend's plate to finalise the tendon and cartilage chewing that he had so casually abandoned.

Just now, recalling her character, I realise she would have delighted in telling this to her friends in the same way I recount my own mothering.

You can thank her for that; I'll thank her for the bone management.

However, these sticks are slippable (yes, that's a word) from their positions, the meat surrounding them rendered beautifully tender and relaxed.

Preheat the oven to 160°C (315°F). Line a large baking dish with foil and baking paper.

A tricky little step here. Flip the ribs and carefully cut away the fine membrane layer that holds the ribs together on the inside. Removing it allows the marinade flavours to get into the meat and also speeds up the tenderisation

of the ribs. The butcher will know how to do this if you don't.

If it doesn't happen, don't worry. Nothing will suffer too badly!

Combine all the marinade ingredients in a large bowl and thoroughly coat the ribs.

Place the ribs in the prepared dish and cover with paper and another layer of foil. Fold and crimp the edges well to seal.

Place in the oven and bake for 2 hours.

In the final 30 minutes of cooking pop the foil potatoes directly on the oven racks.

After 2 hours, remove the top layer of paper and foil from the ribs, and increase the oven temperature to 200°C (400°F). Bake for a further 15 minutes until the edges and tops begin to crisp and char. The spuds should be slightly squishable.

Open the top of the foil parcels and cut deep slits into the spuds (I keep the foil around to catch the sour cream). Top with sour cream and chives and lots of salt.

Eat with the ribs. It's going to get messy.

Serves 4

Sticky Ribs & Foil Spuds

I am a bone cruncher, licker, chewer.
I got that from Mum.

1 cup (155 g) raw
    macadamias, chopped
½ cup (110 g) caster
    (superfine) sugar
1 teaspoon vanilla extract
1 cup (260 g) vanilla-flavoured
    coconut yoghurt
½ cup (125 ml) store-bought
    salted caramel sauce, warmed

MERINGUES
4 large egg whites
⅔ cup (150 g) caster
    (superfine) sugar
1 teaspoon cornflour (cornstarch)
⅓ cup (25 g) shredded coconut

OPTIONAL INGREDIENTS
toasted shredded coconut

THIS HAS ALL THE DESSERT feels for me.

Crispy, airy, sometimes mildly chewy meringue, dollops of silky sweet, softly sour yoghurt, drizzling slicks of caramel and crunchy crystallised sugared nuts.

Oooof.

Preheat the oven to 100°C (200°F). Line two baking trays with baking paper.

To make the meringues, whisk the egg whites in a very clean bowl until stiff peaks form.

Gradually add the sugar, tablespoon by tablespoon, whisking well as you go.

Gently fold in the cornflour and shredded coconut.

Scoop the meringue onto one of the prepared trays in four equal portions. I use a big spoon and aim for a large dollop as the base and a smaller dollop on top. You can push about getting peaks, but given that you will be crushing into the top a bit with yoghurt to serve, you don't need to be too fussy.

Bake for 1½ hours, then turn off the oven and leave them to cool inside, with the door propped slightly open with a wooden spoon. (I also find leaving them in the oven overnight with door fully closed works for me, but it totally depends on the weather. Sometimes the humidity in Sydney can destroy a fluffy day's work in a moment.)

Place the macadamias, sugar and vanilla in a frying pan and toast over medium heat, tossing regularly, for 5–6 minutes until golden and crisp.

Pour onto the second lined tray to cool. Don't worry if the sugar crystallises.

Eat the meringues topped with the coconut vanilla yoghurt, warmed salted caramel and sugared macs.

Serves 4

Coconut Meringues

This may have been described as the best dessert I've ever fed someone.

1 kg (2 lb 3 oz) yellow peaches,
  stones removed, each cut
  into 12 wedges
3 tablespoons rosewater
1 tablespoon vanilla extract
1¼ cups (275 g) caster
  (superfine) sugar
435 g (15½ oz) good-quality
  sweet shortcrust pastry
300 g (10½ oz) thick
  (double) cream

OPTIONAL INGREDIENTS
a flurry of icing (confectioners')
sugar just before serving

MATTEL DID A NUMBER ON me
and I'm not mad about it, even
though this goes against the
teachings of my feminist parents.

Peaches and Cream Barbie is
etched into an ever-evolving
memory that becomes more
elaborate with every dreamy
visual I experience in my life.

A quick Google search reveals
that I actually pretty much stole
her look for my wedding, and
will probably do it again.

This is 'our' outfit as a dessert.

Preheat the oven to 180°C
(350°F). Line a baking tray with
baking paper.

Mix together the peach wedges,
rosewater, vanilla and sugar in
a bowl and leave to macerate
for 30 minutes.

Ball up the pastry, then roll it into
a 40 cm (16 inch) circle and place
on the prepared tray.

Drain the peaches, reserving the
rosy syrup.

Arrange the peaches over the
pastry in a circular pattern,
leaving a 3 cm (1¼ inch) border
around the edge.

Fold in the edges of the pastry.

Bake for 30 minutes until the fruit
is caramelised and the pastry is
cooked and golden.

Meanwhile, pour the reserved
syrup into a small saucepan and
simmer over medium heat until
thickened and reduced by half.
Should take about 5 minutes.
Be careful not to let it burn.

Allow the tart to cool slightly,
then serve with big dollops of
cream and a drizzle of syrup.

Serves 8

Peaches & Cream

Baby dreams come true.

A Chocolate Thing

All my desserts are dream chasers, perhaps because I don't crave them much myself so I rely heavily on that one time …

130 g (4½ oz) butter, melted
1 cup (220 g) sugar
1 teaspoon vanilla extract
3 tablespoons cocoa powder
3 eggs
½ cup (75 g) plain
  (all-purpose) flour
½ cup (55 g) hazelnut meal
1 cup (150 g) roughly chopped
  dark chocolate
10 pink marshmallows

STEWED RHUBARB
1 bunch rhubarb, trimmed and
  cut into 5 cm (2 inch) lengths
3 tablespoons orange juice
½ cup (110 g) sugar
1 cup (110 g) frozen raspberries
  (or fresh if in season)

OPTIONAL INGREDIENTS
vanilla ice cream

I WENT CAMPING at a friend's farm 15 years ago and this one imprinted so heavily that when I texted the group this picture they sent me back an image of a spliff.

Little did we know then that 'stoner's delight' would one day feature regularly on swank restaurant menus.

The blueprint for a dessert of this category is essentially chocolate, then words like warm, gooey, melty, sugary, crisp and chewy, and finally a random 'ooooh yeah let's put this in there!' element. In this case, marshmallows.

Enjoy dudes.

Preheat the oven to 180°C (350°F).

For the stewed rhubarb, combine the rhubarb, orange juice and sugar in a saucepan and simmer over medium heat for 10 minutes until the fruit has softened.

Remove from the heat and stir in the raspberries, then allow the mix to cool.

Whisk together the butter, sugar, vanilla and cocoa powder until light and creamy.

Whisk in the eggs, one at a time.

Gently fold in the flour, hazelnut meal and chocolate until just combined.

Put the rhubarb in the base of a greased ovenproof frying pan (the one I used is 25 cm/ 10 inches) or baking dish and spread evenly. Dot with the marshmallows, and spoon the chocolate batter over the top.

Bake for 30 minutes or until puffed and slightly crispy on the edge.

This can be served a bit underdone, like a self-saucing pudding.

Serves 6

Sunday

Brunch day. With friends or just the day you get to make
a silent little scramble with chilli to eat straight from the pan
alone. Either way, you eat enough in the AM to make it to the PM,
when dinner is comfort in a bowl. Summer fish'n'chips.
Soup. A pie. This is the week's full stop.

2 eggs
1 teaspoon vanilla extract
½ cup (125 ml) single
   (pure) cream
1 day-old baguette, sliced
   diagonally into 1.5 cm (½ inch)
   thick pieces
½ cup (110 g) sugar
1 teaspoon ground cinnamon

OPTIONAL INGREDIENTS
icing (confectioners') sugar,
honey and lemon wedges

MY GOLDEN CHILD* made me this one Mother's Day.

So naturally I took his beautiful gesture of love, redesigned it with some improvements (created a lazier version) and called it my own.

Preheat the oven to 180°C (350°F).

Whisk together the eggs, vanilla and cream.

Place the baguette slices in a single layer in a baking dish lined with baking paper, and pour the egg and cream mixture over the top.

Soak for 5 minutes, then flip over and soak for another 10 minutes. By now, most of the liquid should be absorbed.

Pour the sugar onto a plate. Carefully dip one side of each soggy slice into the sugar, so you have a crusted side.

Wipe any leftover egg and cream mix from the tray, then put the baguette slices back on the paper, sugar-side up.

Dust with cinnamon and bake for 7 minutes.

*Don't freak out. They all get to wear the golden crown and when they do we all bow down, but just for clarity, it's my crown.

Serves 4 (or 1 hungry mumma)

French Baguette Toast

The French and their things: toast, fries, champagne.

massive handful of coarse
 homemade breadcrumbs
 (or just roughly torn bread)
1 tablespoon olive oil
1 tablespoon white wine vinegar
4 eggs
sea salt and freshly ground
 black pepper

HOLLANDAISE
100 g (3½ oz) butter, melted
 and kept warm
2 teaspoons white wine vinegar

1 teaspoon dried tarragon
2 egg yolks

OPTIONAL INGREDIENTS
paracetamol and black coffee

THIS RECIPE IS FOR SELF CARE
any day, anyone with a max laze
but fancy attitude, big-note
brunch hosting, one-night stands
you want to keep around, or
just people like me who tried to
make a traditional hollandaise on
Instagram Live and failed. Twice.

Pan-fry the breadcrumbs with the
oil over medium heat until crispy
and golden. Set aside.

In the same pan, bring 4 cups
(1 litre) of water and the vinegar
to a simmer and poach the eggs.

I am being incredibly nonchalant
about poaching eggs here.
There are a hundred tutorials
online guaranteed to terrify you.
It's likely I will even have posted
one on my YouTube channel
by the time you read this. But
my favourite approach is to just
be ballsy. Crack the eggs with
confidence straight into the pan,
maybe make sure they are not
stuck to the bottom, turn the
heat down a notch and just
wait 5 minutes. Check on them
if you like by lifting them to
see how they're cooking.

Or, if you want to cheat the hell
out of the procedure, just lightly
coat a frying pan in oil and bring
to medium heat, then crack the
eggs in and add 1 cup (250 ml)
of water to kind of water-fry them
like dumplings. It's a strange
alternative I know, but it does
the trick if you can't handle the
anxiety of poaching.

OK, while that's happening,
make the hollandaise. Place
all the ingredients in a small
powerful food blender and blitz
for no more than a few seconds.
You could also use a small stick
blender. The speed/power of the
blend emulsifies the ingredients
in the same way double boiling
and whisking gently does.

Layer the crumbs, poached eggs
and hollandaise on a vessel of
your choosing and in whatever
order you like, season if you want
to, then eat.

Serves 2

Poached Eggs with Crumbs & 30s Hollandaise

Roughly torn pan-fried crumbs are the solution on days when you don't have the strength for sourdough.

300 g (10½ oz) strawberries,
  hulled
1 pink lady apple, cored
  and chopped
4 cups (1 litre) unsweetened
  drinking coconut milk
3 tablespoons maple syrup
1 cup (100 g) rolled oats
1 cup (170 g) chia seeds
1 teaspoon ground cinnamon

OPTIONAL INGREDIENTS
coconut yoghurt, extra maple
syrup, chopped peach and
toasted coconut

IT'S A WEEK OF GOOD STARTS,
ready to go in the fridge.

Jar them individually or just set
it in a big container and scoop
out what you want each day.

Amazingly, the kids love
them too.

Blitz the strawberries and
apple until smooth.

Tip into a large bowl and stir
in the coconut milk, maple syrup,
oats, chia seeds and cinnamon.

Leave the mixture to thicken
for 5 minutes if you're in a hurry,
or overnight if you're being
organised.

Divide among individual jars
(or pile into one big airtight
container) and refrigerate.

Stored this way, they'll keep
for up to 4 days.

Serves 5–6

Strawberry Apple Chia Puddings

You make this on a Sunday evening after you've eaten all the pies and chips and drunk all the drinks.

2 tablespoons veg slap
(see page 210, or buy an
already slapped base)
1 pizza base (store-bought,
naked)
½ cup (65 g) grated mozzarella
4 bacon rashers
1 tablespoon olive oil
3 eggs

OPTIONAL INGREDIENTS
OJ, barbecue sauce and an
outdoor wrestling pit

THIS IS 1000% THE CURE
for almost everything, except
anything too serious.

But also 500% going to be
the cause of tears if you eat it
straight from the oven. Best
eaten outside, near a hose.

Preheat the oven to 200°C (400°F).

Spread the veg slap over the
pizza base.

Cover with mozzarella.

Nestle the bacon into the cheese
so that it peaks up in spots.

Drizzle with the oil.

Bake for 10 minutes until the
cheese has melted.

Remove from the oven and, using
a spoon, make three divots for
the eggs.

Carefully crack the eggs into the
indents of molten lava cheese.

Return to the oven for a further
10 minutes, or until the eggs
are cooked to your liking.

Serves 3 monsters

Breakfast Pizza with Veg Slap

Breakfast. Pizza. Sunday. Done.

2 cups (370 g) leftover cooked jasmine rice
1 tablespoon ghee, melted
sea salt and freshly ground black pepper
5 eggs
1 teaspoon soy sauce
1 tablespoon sesame oil
1 teaspoon grated ginger
1 tablespoon chopped spring onion (scallion)

2 heads of bok choy, halved lengthways (this is pretty, but for an easier eating bowl, roughly chop it)
1 tablespoon fried shallots
1 bird's eye chilli, finely chopped
1 tablespoon chopped coriander (cilantro)
½ cup (60 g) bean sprouts

OPTIONAL INGREDIENTS
black sesame seeds and oyster sauce

DINING OUT FOR BREAKFAST doesn't feel worth it if you don't order from the drink options like a degustation, starting with a coffee, moving to a juice, lining up a second coffee or a pot of tea halfway through eating.

I like to eat the unusual at breakfast. Give me the kedgeree, or the coconut chilli eggs.
Is there a soup on the menu before 10.30 am? Yes please.

But this kind of confusion is rarely available. So I often flex it out at home on a Sunday.

Toss the rice in the liquid ghee until evenly coated. Season well.

Pat the rice evenly into the base of a 20 cm (8 inch) frying pan and fry over medium heat for about 15 minutes until you can tell it's crisp by looking at the top.

Combine the eggs, soy, sesame oil, ginger and spring onion until they are lightly scrambled.

Remove the crispy rice cake from the pan … it will break into shards*.

Pan-fry the bok choy over high heat for 2 minutes without turning it, and remove.

Reduce the heat to low and pour in the egg mixture. Cook, folding gently as the edges and base set, for about 5 minutes. I stop just before it is completely set, letting the residual heat finish it off.

Serve the scrambled egg with crunchy rice shards, bok choy, fried shallots, chilli, coriander and bean sprouts.

*Please, if you were not raised on water with toxic fluoride levels or just generally don't have strong teeth, just fry the rice like a stir-fry to heat it through and give it some personality. Do not attempt to eat the rice crisp … your teeth WILL fall apart.

Serves 2

Rice Crunch Scramble

This is a holiday on a plate for me.
Preferably eaten by the pool at 9.30 am,
followed by an 11 am G&T, then a nap.

Toasted Carbs
Stuffed with Stuff x 3

These have all the qualities you look for in a support partner: speed, salt, chew, goo, crisp. There's a window of perfection 6 minutes after they're made that lasts for 10 minutes EXACTLY. Either side of that and you'll either have a seared chin or a deflated sense of self, and you should probably just go back to eating your kids' discarded crusts from the bench or car. I have pondered making these ahead and freezing them, but then I'd have to defrost some other intention in the freezer to make room.

Egg & Bacon Burrito

olive oil spray
2 eggs
1 wholegrain burrito
2 streaky bacon rashers, fried
1 small leftover cooked potato,
   chopped and fried (pretty
   much any cooked spud from
   this book is the perfect one!)
3 tablespoons grated cheddar
1 tablespoon barbecue sauce

Spray a frying pan with oil and
heat over medium–high heat.

Add the eggs and break the
yolk with the shell.

Top with the burrito, gently
pressing the egg to the edge.

Cook for 5 minutes.

Remove to a board, egg-side up.

Top with the bacon, potato,
cheese and barbecue sauce.

Roll it up and put it back in the
pan for 3 minutes each side until
golden and melty.

Wrap + run.

Serves 1

Kraut & Chilli On Rye

2 slices of rye bread
4 slices of mozzarella
3 tablespoons sauerkraut
1 teaspoon sriracha
sea salt and freshly ground
   black pepper
kewpie mayonnaise,
   for spreading
olive oil spray

Top one slice of bread with half
the mozzarella, the sauerkraut,
sriracha, salt and pepper, and
the rest of the mozza. Sandwich
with the other slice of bread.

Butter the outside of the
sandwich with the mayo.

Heat a lightly oiled non-stick
frying pan over medium–high
heat.

Fry the sandwich for 4 minutes
each side to melt the cheese.

Grab + go.

Serves 1

Cheese & Spinach Gozleme

1 Greek pita wrap
3 tablespoons fresh ricotta
baby fist of baby spinach
2 tablespoons grated haloumi
sea salt and freshly ground
   black pepper
1 tablespoon olive oil
squeeze of lemon juice

Heat a frying pan over
medium–high heat.

Put the pita in the pan for
1 minute to soften.

Remove to a board and spread
ricotta on one half.

Top the ricotta with the spinach,
haloumi, salt and pepper, then
fold in half.

Put the pan back over medium–
high heat and heat the oil.

Fry the gozleme for 3 minutes
each side to wilt the spinach.

Finish with a squeeze of lemon
juice.

Slice + split.

Serves 1

CONGEE

½ cup (25 g) chopped coriander (cilantro)
1 whole 1.2 kg (2 lb 10 oz) chicken (go with free-range and organic for this one)
2 onions, peeled and quartered
3 large carrots, chopped into 3 cm (1¼ inch) chunks
1 celery stick, chopped
10 cm (4 inch) knob of ginger, roughly chopped
5 cm (2 inch) knob of turmeric, halved

at least 8 cups (2 litres) cold water (enough to generously cover the chicken)
1 tablespoon chicken stock powder
1 head of cauliflower, chunky chopped
1 tablespoon sea salt
1½ cups (315 g) brown rice
1 tablespoon sesame oil
2 tablespoons mirin

SEASONING

grated ginger
fresh and fried shallots
sesame oil
Chinese black vinegar
soy sauce
sea salt

OPTIONAL INGREDIENTS

chunky chopped chilli

THIS IS LOW AND SLOW.

Don't plan anything too stressful. Or if you are stressed, make this the focus of the day – see it as a form of meditation.

You can go out for an hour, but then you need to return to this.

This is your project today … and it will nourish you the same way the warmest and most robust hug would do.

And here's the best bit.

Put all the ingredients for the congee in a stockpot and time does the rest (sort of).

Bring to a very gentle simmer. Keep the lid off.

After about an hour, remove the chicken and set aside until it's cool enough to handle.

Shred the chicken meat from the bones and set it aside until you're ready to serve.

Crack a few larger bones and put them back in the pot for another hour, but count them first because the sump-like nature of

a congee is not going to make fishing easy.

I also finely shred the skin and slide that back into the brew.

Stir occasionally to make sure it's not catching.

The rice will break down and the cauliflower will eventually resemble rice.

If you like, you can stretch out this cathartic process for up to 3 hours.

Remove what bones you can find (or do it as you serve). If you want to clean it all up, remove the turmeric and ginger chunks too.

Thinly slice the ginger and put it back in, along with the shredded chicken, and reheat before serving.

You have now reached seasoning time. Add any or all of the following: grated ginger, fresh and fried shallots, sesame oil, black vinegar, soy sauce and salt. Make it yours.

Serves 6–8

Chicken Cauliflower Congee

This is the perfect care parcel to deliver to a friend, and the perfect smell for a house on a rainy day.

1 kg (2 lb 3 oz) desiree potatoes
2 tablespoons olive oil
1 teaspoon fine salt
½ cup (75 g) plain
   (all-purpose) flour
sea salt and freshly ground
   black pepper
1 egg
1½ cups (90 g) panko
   breadcrumbs
500 g (1 lb 2 oz) firm white
   fish fillets, skin removed
   and pin-boned, cut into
   5 cm (2 inch) chunks

olive oil spray
2 bunches asparagus,
   ends snapped off
¾ cup (110 g) frozen peas
butter, for tossing

TARTARE SAUCE
½ cup (120 g) mayonnaise
3 tablespoons finely chopped dill
1 tablespoon capers
2–3 cornichons, chopped

OPTIONAL INGREDIENTS
lemon wedges

HAVE YOU EVER NOTICED

that once you hear someone say fush and chups, you start saying it that way for a brief period afterwards?

Every accent must have one word or phrase that has this effect on people.

This is New Zealand's.

Australia's would be a nasal 'aw, yeah, naaaah'.

This must not be eaten with cutlery or even plates, but off paper, and technically you should be sitting on the floor or grass while you eat it.

Preheat the oven to 200°C (400°F).

Cut the potatoes into 1 cm (½ inch) thick chips. Rinse and pat dry.

Toss the chips in the oil and salt, and spread out on a non-stick baking tray.

Bake for 15 minutes, then turn them over and bake for another 25 minutes.

To prep the fish, tip the flour into one bowl and season well, beat the egg in a second bowl, and tip the panko crumbs into a third.

Lightly dust the fish in flour, then dip in the egg and toss in the panko crumbs to coat.

Place the fish on a separate tray in a single layer and spray lightly with oil. Pop in the oven for the last 15 minutes of the chip cooking time.

To make the tartare sauce, combine all the ingredients in a small bowl.

Just before the fush and chups are ready, blanch the asparagus and peas. I just put them in a heatproof bowl, pour over some boiling water and leave them for a few minutes.

Drain and toss with butter.

Serves 2 big or 4 small appetites

Crumbed Fish, Chips & Peas

Sunday fish and chips is a solid farewell to whatever you did that weekend.

olive oil, for pan-frying
1 onion, diced
sea salt and freshly ground
  black pepper
3 carrots, diced
1 celery stick, diced
4 sprigs rosemary, leaves
  stripped
4 garlic cloves, crushed
1 kg (2 lb 3 oz) chuck beef,
  cut into 3 cm (1¼ inch) cubes
⅓ cup (50 g) plain
  (all-purpose) flour

1 cup (250 ml) red wine
2 cups (200 g) chopped swiss
  brown mushrooms
1 teaspoon porcini powder
2 cups (500 ml) beef stock
3 potatoes, pierced
2 sweet potatoes, pierced
2 cups (500 ml) beshy
  (see page 204)
½ cup (125 ml) milk
2 cups (200 g) grated cheddar

OPTIONAL INGREDIENTS
broccolini (or other lovely dark
green veg), sauteed with garlic,
olive oil and salt

WE DON'T MAKE ENOUGH

individual pies, mainly because
they are so easy to buy.

But they are supremely
comforting, especially when
eaten at home.

The whole process of consuming
them requires a snuggling
mentality.

Heat a splash of oil in a large
ovenproof frying pan or flameproof
casserole dish over medium heat,
add the onion and 1 tablespoon
of salt and fry for 5 minutes.

Add the carrot, celery and
rosemary and fry for 5 minutes.

Add the garlic and fry for another
5 minutes.

Remove the veg mixture from the
pan and wipe out any burnt bits.

Toss the beef in the flour to
lightly coat.

Heat some more oil in the
pan over high heat. Working
in batches, brown the beef for
2 minutes each side until golden
but not cooked through.

Transfer the beef to a plate and
season well.

Deglaze the pan with the red wine.

Add the vegetable mixture, along
with the mushroom and porcini
powder, and stir well.

Return the beef to the pan and
pour in the stock.

Cover with a cartouche (a piece
of baking paper cut to fit the
pan) and a lid, and cook over
medium heat for 2 hours until the
meat is tender and the sauce has
reduced and thickened.

Allow to cool.

Put the potatoes and sweet
potatoes in a microwave-safe
container that has a lid with a vent
(you don't want this completely
sealed). Zap for 4 minutes, then cut
into 5 mm (¼ inch) thick slices.

Make the beshy, adding the extra
milk and cheese.

Preheat the oven to 180°C (350°F).

To make the pies, divide the
beef filling among six individual

ovenproof dishes. Pour over the
cheesy beshy and finish with an
overlapping layer of potato and
sweet potato.

Brush with oil and season.

Bake for 40 minutes.

Serves 6

Beef & Potato Top Pies

I couldn't decide which beef pie to include, and then I remembered on Sunday I want ALL of them in one.

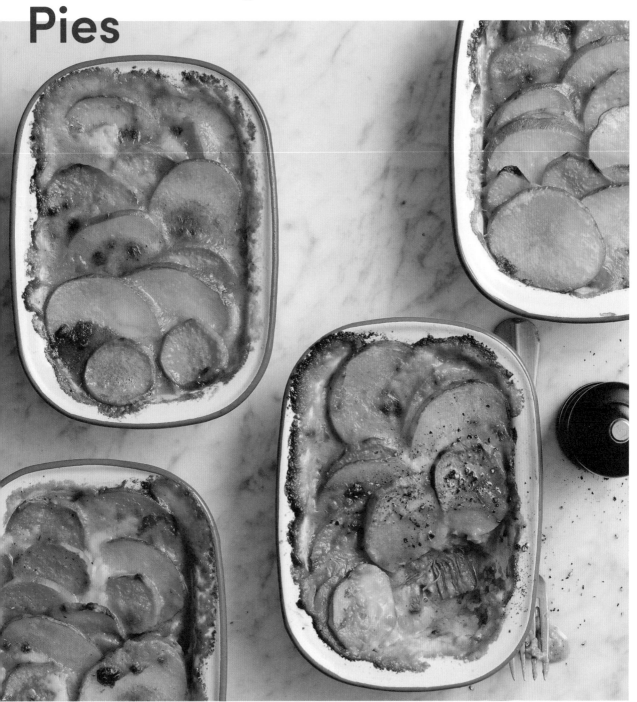

Roast Tomato Soup with Rosemary & Cheese Flatties

I love soup so much that if it was on a breakfast menu, I would choose it immediately. On that note, can some one please do this? Stat!

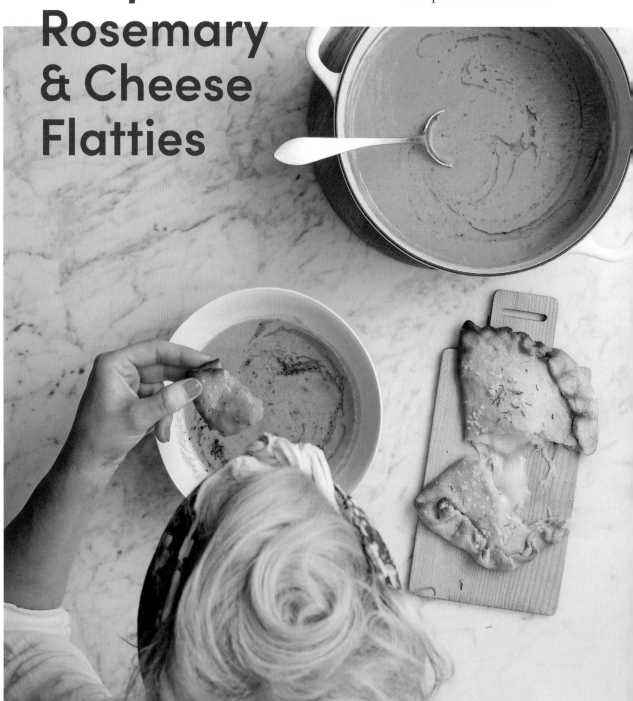

8 roma tomatoes, halved
  lengthways
1 leek, white and pale green
  part only, sliced into 1 cm
  (½ inch) thick rounds
3 tablespoons oregano leaves
1 teaspoon sea salt, plus extra
  for sprinkling
1 teaspoon freshly ground
  black pepper
3 tablespoons olive oil
2 cups (500 ml) chicken stock

100 ml (3½ fl oz) thick
  (double) cream
1 quantity of yoghurt flatty
  dough* (see page 212)
2 cups (200 g) grated cheddar
2 teaspoons dried rosemary

OPTIONAL INGREDIENTS
chilli flakes and parmy

MY FAMILY ARE IDIOTS ABOUT SOUP.

It's as if, despite my best efforts, they can't translate liquid food into something you need to swallow. Instead it seems to dribble out of their face.

Perhaps our eating-with-mouths-closed policy is a bit relaxed.

Perhaps they see me make too many green smoothies to trust what's in it.

Perhaps we need to have more egg'n'spoon races so they grasp the concept of a spoon.

Either way, it doesn't deter me.

Preheat the oven to 180°C (350°F).

Massage the tomato, leek, oregano, salt and pepper with half the oil in a bowl.

Spread out on a baking tray lined with baking paper and roast for 30 minutes.

Combine the roast tomato mix (including all the pan juices) with the stock in a medium saucepan and bring to a simmer.

Stir through the cream, then remove from the heat.

Use a stick blender to puree the soup while hot, or wait until it cools and blend in an upright blender, then reheat.

While the tomatoes are roasting, divide the dough into four balls.

Roll each ball into a circle about 1 cm (½ inch) thick.

Place ½ cup (50 g) of cheese on one half of each circle, leaving a 1 cm (½ inch) edge.

Fold the dough over the cheese and clumsily crump/fold/mash/seal the dough edges.

Place on a large baking tray lined with baking paper, brush with the remaining oil and sprinkle with salt and rosemary.

As soon as you have removed the tomatoes from the oven, crank the heat up to 200°C (400°F).

Once the oven has reached temperature, bake the flatbreads for 20 minutes.

Divvy up the soft and comforting soup with the cheesy chewy flatties and enjoy.

Freeze the soup they don't eat and save it for yourself.

*Or use pre-made fresh dough, available from the refrigerated section at larger supermarkets.

Serves 4

Pork Belly & Baby Food

If you've got kids and have ever stared aimlessly at the food in the baby aisle, you probably already know this one.

2 kg (4 lb 6 oz) pork belly, scored and salted, left to rest uncovered in the fridge overnight
olive oil, for drizzling
generous bowl of baby food (pureed apple or pear)

RED CABBAGE SALAD
2 tablespoons olive oil
1 red onion, sliced
5 garlic cloves, smashed
4 cups (300 g) shredded red cabbage

1 cup (200 g) grated or thinly sliced red apple
6 sprigs thyme, leaves stripped (or left whole if the stalks are tender)
2 tablespoons seeded mustard
1 tablespoon brown sugar
2 tablespoons red wine vinegar

OPTIONAL INGREDIENTS
chilli flakes and sea salt

PUREED PEAR AND APPLE

from the petite meal aisle is the second greatest baby food hack to cure a hangover.

The first of course is apple and redcurrant jelly.

Despite my kids all being old enough to use a tin opener I still buy both of these products.

The jar size is appropriate, the sugar is just what's in the fruit and there aren't any of the weird stabilising additives you often find in apple sauce aimed at a more mature palate.

To obtain ultimate crackle you really need to prep the skin. Scoring the skin is about opening the top layer so the fat can run out during cooking, without cutting into the meat at all. Your butcher can do this for you (some more carefully than others!), otherwise use a very sharp knife or a scalpel and ruler. Then pour a kettle full of boiling water over the skin to open the cracks. Pat dry, rub with salt and leave to dry uncovered in the fridge overnight.

The next day, rinse and pat dry the skin, lightly oil and re-salt. Bring the meat to room temp before cooking (30 mins or so).

Preheat the oven to 240°C (475°F).

Rinse the pork and pat dry, then drizzle with olive oil.

Place in a roasting tin, skin-side up, and roast for 20 minutes to get the crackling going. Turn the oven down to 150°C (300°F) and roast for another 1½ hours.

Meanwhile, for the cabbage salad, heat the oil in a frying pan over medium heat. Saute the onion and garlic for 5 minutes.

Add the red cabbage, apple, thyme and mustard and cook for another 5 minutes. Stir in the sugar and cook for 3 minutes.

Finally, add the red wine vinegar and cook for 2 minutes.

Serve the pork with crackling, cabbage salad and baby food.

Serves 6

That extra day you wished for

If Beyoncé gets an extra day (and she does, I'm telling you) then so do we. And if not a day, then at least an hour. Or just a few minutes, damn it. These little numbers will keep you prancing, with glee or fury.

2 cups (500 ml) olive oil
8 garlic cloves, peeled
   and gently bruised
1 parmesan rind

OPTIONAL INGREDIENTS
you can of course drink this neat,
however saturating some sort of
carb is my preferred method
of consumption

A PLAIN PARMY OIL felt like it
would be a bit like Kramer when
he got his own show (just a bit
offputting and pointless) so
I make it with its one true love:
garlic (Seinfeld).

Place the oil and garlic in a
saucepan over EXTREMELY low
heat for 1 hour.

If you have a gas stovetop
I recommend putting it in a
baking dish in a 120°C (235°F)
oven for an hour (make sure the
garlic is covered).

Allow to cool, then discard the
garlic cloves and pour the oil into
an airtight container. Add the
parmesan rind and store in the
fridge for 1–2 weeks.

Makes 2 cups (500 ml)

Garlic Parmy Oil

I started doing this because we eat parmy in excess and I can't bear to chuck out the rinds.

½ cup (125 ml) lemon juice
1 garlic clove, peeled and smashed (into big chunks you can fish out later)
2 tablespoons dijon mustard
2 teaspoons sugar
2 teaspoons sea salt
½ cup (50 g) grated parmesan
1 cup (250 ml) extra virgin olive oil (EVO oil)

OPTIONAL INGREDIENTS
fresh herbs, chilli, other mustards and anchovies

GOOGLE 'STORING SALAD DRESSINGS' and there are lots of opinions: *'lemon juice goes gross'*, *'NEVER refrigerate EVO oil'* etc.

These may all be true and my palate may very well be unsophisticated, but I have a jar of this running like master stock in my fridge for weeks.

It gets low fast and I top it up with stuff.

You can decide if that works for you but the main thing is to remove the raw garlic.

If you want to leave it in there, then saute it first.

Lemon juice + garlic + dijon + sugar + salt + parmesan > a jar or bowl.

Leave for 30 minutes.

Walk away.

Make dinner. Pour a drink. Talk to your guests. Play a round of Pictionary with your kids where all they draw is a stick man even if they get the word 'carwash'.

The key is to let the lemon juice dissolve, cook and suck the deliciousness out of everything in that mix. Just go away long enough to suddenly think 'Oh, the salad dressing!'.

Add the EVO oil and shake or whisk like crazy.

Learn this. You will use this dressing often. Here are some things I do with it:

• Halve the quantities and make it in the base of the large bowl you plan to serve a big green salad in. Tossing dressing from the bottom up is enlightening.

• Add chives.

• Add basil and some smooshed roasted cherry toms.

• Toss it through a zucchini pasta with ricotta.

• Combine some with an equal amount of mayonnaise and mix with a shredded roast chook for the easiest picnic roll filling.

• Add a tablespoon to your scrambled egg mix.

• Mash with anchovies and butter to eat on toast.

Makes a bit over 1½ cups (375 ml)

Vinai-no-regrette (Vinaigrette)

My grandmother would always say a salad should be tossed with conviction. This is conviction.

Pickled Carrot

4 carrots, peeled and julienned
2 tablespoons fine salt
½ cup (110 g) caster
    (superfine) sugar
2 cups (500 ml) white vinegar
2 coriander (cilantro) roots, split
2 star anise

Toss the carrot in the salt and allow to sit for 10 minutes.

Meanwhile, bring the sugar, vinegar, coriander root and star anise to a simmer until the sugar has dissolved. Turn off the heat and allow to cool a bit.

Rinse the salt off the carrot and place in a large jar. Pour in the warm pickling liquid and leave to pickle for at least an hour before you eat it. Store in the fridge for up to a week.

Fills a 500 ml (17 fl oz) jar

Poke Zen Dressing

1 teaspoon honey
1 teaspoon rice wine vinegar
½ cup (125 ml) mirin
3 tablespoons soy sauce
⅓ cup (80 ml) orange juice
1 tablespoon sesame oil
1 tablespoon grated ginger
2 tablespoons sliced spring
    onion (scallion)
1 teaspoon sesame seeds

If the honey is looking a bit solid, warm it slightly to loosen.

Place all the ingredients in a jar and shake well to combine.

Store in the fridge for up to a week.

Makes about 1½ cups (375 ml)

G-rated Nuoc Cham

3 tablespoons fish sauce
3 tablespoons rice wine vinegar
2 tablespoons sugar
2 garlic cloves, smashed
2 tablespoons lime juice
½ cup (70 g) cherry tomatoes

Place all the ingredients in a blender, add ½ cup (125 ml) of water and blend to your desired chunkiness. Store in the fridge for up to a week.

Makes about 450 ml (15 fl oz)

Asian-inspired Good Stuff

You'll be tempted to drink these.
And you should.

Baked Coconut Rice

2 cups (400 g) jasmine rice
1 tablespoon olive oil
2 tablespoons shredded coconut
3 cups (750 ml) chicken stock

Preheat the oven to 200°C (400°F).

Rinse the rice three times or until the water runs clear.

Heat the oil in an ovenproof frying pan over medium heat, add the rice and stir until well coated.

Add the coconut and chicken stock and stir well.

Place in the oven and bake for around 30 minutes, or until the rice is tender.

The result here is more indulgent in flavour and texture – a bit of overcooking in the centre with chewy and crispy edges.

Serves 6 as a side

Steamed Stove Rice

2 cups (400 g) jasmine rice
1 tablespoon olive oil

Have a saucepan with a tight-fitting lid ready.

Rinse the rice three times or until the water runs clear.

Tip it into the saucepan, add the oil and toss to make sure the rice is well coated.

Pour in 3 cups (750 ml) of water. Bring to the boil over high heat.

Reduce the heat to medium and simmer for 10 minutes or until almost all the water has been absorbed and little crab holes form in the rice.

Reduce the heat to low.

Wrap the lid in a clean tea towel and cover the rice.

Cook gently for 10 minutes more, until the rice is tender.

The result is fluffy, delicate clean-tasting rice. I usually double this and freeze some for fried rice.

Serves 6 as a side

Rice, Top and Bottom

As with most things, I really can't work out which way I prefer it.

Thai inspired

1 tablespoon shrimp paste
  in oil
1 onion, roughly chopped
2 garlic cloves, chopped
1 stick lemongrass, white part
  only, finely chopped
2 sprigs coriander (cilantro),
  finely chopped
3 makrut lime leaves, spine
  removed and leaves torn
3 cm (1¼ inch) knob of
  galangal, grated
½ teaspoon coriander
  seeds, ground
½ teaspoon cumin
  seeds, ground
½ cup (100 g) chargrilled
  capsicum (pepper)

Blend all the ingredients until
smooth.

Store in an airtight container in
the fridge for a week or freeze in
small portions for up to 4 months.

Makes about 1 cup (250 g)

Indian inspired

80 g (2½ oz) ghee
1 onion, roughly chopped
5 cm (2 inch) knob of
  ginger, grated
10 fresh curry leaves
1 teaspoon cumin
  seeds, ground
1 tablespoon ground turmeric
1 teaspoon coriander
  seeds, ground
1 teaspoon yellow
  mustard seeds
1 tablespoon tamarind paste
1 teaspoon ground cinnamon
1 tablespoon garam marsala

Blend all the ingredients until
smooth.

Store in an airtight container in
the fridge for a week or freeze in
small portions for up to 4 months.

Makes about 1 cup (250 g)

G-rated Curry Pastes

Like watching *Deadpool*, but without the violent spice and sex scenes.

flesh from 2 avocados
3 tablespoons lime juice
baby fist of coriander (cilantro) leaves, chopped
1–2 tablespoons jalapeno chillies (depending on how much heat you like)
1 tablespoon olive oil
1 tablespoon sea salt
2 spring onions (scallions), chopped

OPTIONAL INGREDIENTS
it will tell you what it goes with, don't worry!

BLEND EVERYTHING until smooth. Store in the fridge for up to a week.

I know. What a ridiculous recipe.

But it won't be once you've tried it.

To make a non-spicy version, remove the chilli but replace it with 1 tablespoon of white wine vinegar.

Makes 1½ cups (375 ml)

Spicy Goddess (Avocado & Jalapeno Dressing)

This is a lovely pale green colour, which I instantly want to smear on my face.

100 g (3½ oz) butter
½ cup (75 g) plain
    (all-purpose) flour
4 cups (1 litre) milk, plus extra
    if needed
¼ teaspoon grated nutmeg
1 bay leaf
1 tablespoon sea salt
1 teaspoon ground white pepper

OPTIONAL INGREDIENTS
black pepper (I bought white
pepper for this ONE instance
and have never located the jar
since; I have also not missed it)
and a desire to make lasagne,
nachos or just bathe in it

SOME MILDLY INVIGORATING
crap I've done to beshy includes
adding tonnes of cheese, or
cayenne pepper, or creamed
corn even. (I did all of these
things when I catered a friend's
bucks party and layered it into a
strange hot bean dip. They either
absolutely loved it or were so
stoned they would have eaten a
pan-fried cow pat if I seasoned it
well enough. Who knows?)

OK, in a big saucepan* over
medium–low heat, melt the
butter and allow it to just start
foaming.

Add the flour and stir it into
a paste with a wooden spoon.

It should be smooth and
golden. Imagine you want
EVERY particle of flour to have
its own meticulously applied
layer of body oil.

Reduce the heat to low and add
the milk, 1 cup (250 ml) at a time.

The first cup will instantly plug
everything up. Keep stirring and
try and get it back to a smooth
state before adding more.

I switch to a whisk about now,
or after the next cup – once it's
loose enough to accept a whisk.

It will help you keep the mixture
smooth.

Gradually add the rest of the
milk, whisking between each
addition.

Stop once you have a lovely
thick, smooth texture. It may
continue to thicken as it cooks
and the flour swells more, but
you can just add more milk
to your liking.

It's easier to loosen than it is
to re-thicken so go slow.

Bechamel is traditionally
seasoned with nutmeg, bay
leaves, salt and white pepper.
But you do you.

I also read (skimmed over)
an article online (and didn't
investigate) that claimed this
'sauce' originated in Italy, yet it
is known as one of the 'mother
sauces' of French cuisine.

I just put this in so you can start
a pompous conversation next
time you are eating macaroni
and cheese.

That's it. You've done a beshy!
Now start imagining all the
wonderful things you can dip into
it, drown in it, bake under it or
layer it with.

---

*Aim for a 4 litre pan because even though
the yield is only 1 litre, you will be stirring
hot thick liquid, sometimes quickly, so it
pays to have much higher sides!

*Makes 4 cups (1 litre – just halve
the quantities if this is too much)*

Beshy (Bechamel)

This deserves its own recipe because once you make it well once, you'll start doing weird and exciting crap to it.

4 bunches basil (about 10 cups,
   loosely packed)
½ cup (80 g) pine nuts, lightly
   toasted and cooled
1½ cups (150 g) finely grated
   pecorino and parmesan,
   loosely packed
2 teaspoons sea salt
1 cup (250 ml) extra virgin
   olive oil
2 tablespoons lemon juice

1 teaspoon freshly ground
   black pepper
1 garlic clove, crushed

OPTIONAL INGREDIENTS
a Tuscan villa

AS SOON AS SUMMER hits,
you should make a batch.

This one is perfectly salty
and tangy.

A couple of tips before
you start:

1. To soften the flavour, poach
the garlic clove in milk for a few
minutes first. It's essential to the
umaminess of pesto, but some
people can't deal with it raw.

2. To make it the ultimate green,
dunk the basil into boiling water
then immediately put it in iced
water to shock it. Pat off the
excess water, then proceed
with the recipe.

This is so straightforward,
as with most slurries.

Put everything in a food
processor and blend to your
desired level of smoothness
or chunkiness.

Make sure it's covered in oil
before you pop it in the fridge,
where it will keep for 2 weeks.
Otherwise you can freeze it in
ice-cube trays, then store the
little pesto cubes in zip-lock bags
in the freezer.

Makes 2 cups (500 g)

Pesto

This is the jarred supermarket sauce that seriously needs to get f*cked.

Herb Slurry

100 g (3½ oz) leftover herbs
(flat-leaf or curly parsley,
mint, basil, dill, coriander,
oregano, chives)
2 cups (500 ml) olive oil
1 tablespoon sea salt

OPTIONAL INGREDIENTS
to make it a bit more salsa
verde: 1 tablespoon dijon
mustard, 1 teaspoon grated
lemon zest, 1 teaspoon red
wine vinegar and a pinch of
chilli flakes

Blend everything together until
smooth. Store in a jar in the
fridge for up to 2 weeks, or freeze
in ice-cube trays for 3 months.

Makes about 2 cups (500 ml)

Herb Butter

100 g (3½ oz) leftover herbs
(curly or flat-leaf parsley,
rosemary, oregano, thyme)
baby fist of spring onions
(scallions)
2 garlic cloves, peeled
250 g (9 oz) butter, at room
temperature

OPTIONAL INGREDIENTS
to make it a bit more Cafe de
Paris: 6 anchovies, 1 tablespoon
capers and 1 teaspoon grated
lemon zest

Blend the herbs, spring onion
and garlic until finely chopped.

Add the butter to the herbs and
pulse until just combined. Finish
mixing by hand in a small bowl
so you don't overblend and the
butter doesn't melt too much.

Place on a piece of baking paper
or plastic wrap and roll into a log.

Store in an airtight container in
the fridge for up to 2 weeks, or
freeze for 3 months.

Makes a 350 g (12½ oz) log

Slurry & Butter

Never throw away herbs. You're not the
Wolf of Wall Street.

Veg Slap

This recipe is ideal for getting more veg into the faces and bloodstreams of your children.

1 onion, skin on, chopped
2 zucchini (courgettes)
1 carrot
3 tomatoes
1 red capsicum (pepper),
   halved and seeded
2 tablespoons olive oil
1 tablespoon sea salt
1 tablespoon sugar
2 teaspoons oregano leaves
4 garlic cloves
400 g (14 oz) tin tomatoes

OPTIONAL INGREDIENTS
smugness

THIS IS ALSO HANDY for hiding
that excess quantity of market-
day produce you excitedly
bought and were subsequently
accused of letting go to waste.

Slap is just that. You slap it on
pizza bases. Into sambos. On
tortellini. With grilled meat.

Preheat the oven to 180°C (350°F).

Massage everything except the
tinned tomatoes together in
a baking dish.

Roast for 40 minutes.

Remove any tough skins or stalks
and then blitz with the tinned
tomatoes.

Jar > Eat / Freeze / Sell / Gift.

Keeps well in the fridge for up to
4 days, or freeze for 3 months.

Makes 2 cups (500 ml)

3⅓ cups (500 g)
    self-raising flour
2 cups (520 g) Greek-
    style yoghurt
3 tablespoons olive oil
1 tablespoon sea salt

OPTIONAL INGREDIENTS
1 sachet dried yeast and
the world is your oyster,
although I have not actually
had this with oysters

THIS IS A STAPLE at our place for a few reasons.

It is easy, quick and you don't have to let it rise or rest if you need to work fast.

It has a lovely soft texture when cooked that appeals to kids who feel crusts are akin to concrete.

Sift the flour* into a bowl, and then combine with all the other ingredients**.

Once you've created a gluey uneven mess, turn it out onto a floured surface and knead it until it is smooth and even. This is a fast knead, just a lovely romantic moment between you and the dough … no longer than a flirty pause really.

Place the dough in an oiled bowl and cover with plastic wrap or a silicon lid. Something airtight. Put it in a warm place and try to rest it for at least 30 minutes so that the glutens in the flour can relax and become one with the yoghurt***.

Now roll it out and do WTF you want with it.

Pizzas
Roti
Flatties
Foldovers

You can bake or fry it too!

Hot from the pan, the flatbreads are delicious with a drizzle of oil, extra salt, chilli flakes and some garlic powder.

For a fun curry dunker, change the flour to wholemeal, add sliced spring onion (scallion) to the mix and roll it super thin.

Go wild, my friends.

---

*Full disclosure: I rarely do this, but professional chefs/bakers have been making this step one in recipes for centuries and I can't afford the backlash of being the first to publish that it's unnecessary.

**Add the yeast here too if you are after a puffy pizza dough!

***Not a baker so the terminology will be off here, but the ingredients essentially need time to 'Netflix & chill'.

Makes enough for 2 x 40 cm (16 inch) pizzas or about 8 x 15 cm (6 inch) flatbreads

Yoghurt Flatty Dough

This dough is so easy to make, then you roll it out and do WTF you want with it.

Sprinkles x 3

Your life will be infinitely better if you invest in a little sprinkle production.

Soy Sunflower Seeds

1 tablespoon soy sauce
2 makrut lime leaves, thinly sliced
1 tablespoon maple syrup
1½ cups (220 g) sunflower seeds
1 tablespoon kecap manis

Preheat the oven to 200°C (400°F). Line a baking tray with baking paper.

Combine all the ingredients and spread out on the prepared tray.

Bake for 2–3 minutes.

Cool completely, then store in an airtight container for up to a week.

Makes about 300 g (10½ oz)

Pangrattato

1 cup (60 g) fresh breadcrumbs
2 anchovies, chopped
½ teaspoon chilli flakes
1 cup (100 g) grated parmesan
1 tablespoon rosemary leaves
1 tablespoon olive oil

Combine everything and toast in a frying pan or the oven until crisp and golden.

Store in an airtight container in the fridge for up to a week, or freeze for 3 months.

Makes about 2 cups (120 g)

Gremolata

1 cup (20 g) curly parsley
1 tablespoon grated lemon zest
1 garlic clove
sea salt

Chop fine, combine.

Store in an airtight container in the fridge for up to a week.

Makes about 1 cup (25 g)

Thank you

I've never felt more surrounded by great people.

To start, I acknowledge the Traditional Owners of Country throughout Australia, the Gadigal people of the Eora Nation, and recognise their continuing connection to land, waters and culture. I would like to pay my respects to their Elders past, present and emerging.

My daily team. While it is true that I wrote, tested, styled and photographed this book, I couldn't have done it without this team of women: Collette, Sarah, Katja, Emma and Vikki-Leigh. They took it in shifts to accompany me – cooking by my side, guiding the stream of consciousness that spilt from my mind, pressing capture every now and then, recommending manicures, providing hideaway spaces to write, and dismantling my imposter syndrome by eating everything on these pages with audible pleasure.

My intelligence dept. Aka, a collection of incredible photographers who have patiently educated me, generously loaned me equipment, fielded ridiculous questions and graciously shared their time and space with me so I could shoot this book (quite possibly because the threat level here is incredibly low): William, Hannah, Cath, Chris and Simon.

My IP security team, Joe & Ben. Who made me go slow when all I wanted to do was race, and have helped me re-imagine business as pleasure.

My publishing team at Murdoch Books. Jane, who reached out and encouraged me to bring my real personality (and voice) to print from the very beginning, along with Megan, VB, Rachel and Kirby. They have made this a reality, so you can @ them. Thank you MB team for 'getting' me!

My suppliers. The shops in my 'hood that support small and seasonal farming, whose staff love what they do and have become great friends of mine (some have even been allocated speed-dial spots on my phone ... sorry, not sorry): Peter's Meats Maroubra, Fresh Point Deli and The Fish Market @ Maroubra. Plus the artisans, makers and creators of the beautiful bits and pieces you'll see throughout this book, who are passionate about the continued success of food in print media: akeramic, Cultiver, Studio Enti and Major & Tom.

And of course the ENOTW Instagram community. What's mine is yours (not royalties or license but you know what I mean). Without your encouragement, swearing, proofreading, under-the-influence DMs, laughing, crying and sharing ... I probably wouldn't bother. Thank you x

My husband, Andrew, who looks after the kids, the house, the budgets, the pets, just like a parent and partner should when the other is busy, so whenever I was asked, 'Who is looking after the kids while you work such long hours on this book?' I didn't have to panic and phone a storage unit to check child maintenance routines. You have been the most incredible support to me and my ideas. I love you.

My kids, James, Beau and Winter. Thank you my darling hearts for providing constant fodder for my writing, the severest of reality checks and the sweetest-smelling comfort in all your cuddles. Even if it was when you needed me ... I feel like I get WAY more out of it.

Index

Published in 2021 by Murdoch Books, an imprint of Allen & Unwin

Murdoch Books Australia
83 Alexander Street
Crows Nest NSW 2065
Phone: +61 (0)2 8425 0100
murdochbooks.com.au
info@murdochbooks.com.au

Murdoch Books UK
Ormond House
26–27 Boswell Street
London WC1N 3JZ
Phone: +44 (0) 20 8785 5995
murdochbooks.co.uk
info@murdochbooks.co.uk

For corporate orders and custom publishing, contact our business development team at
salesenquiries@murdochbooks.com.au

Publisher: Jane Morrow
Editorial Manager: Virginia Birch
Design Manager: Megan Pigott
Designer: Kirby Armstrong
Editor: Rachel Carter
Concept, recipes, art direction, styling and photography: Lucy Tweed
Additional photography: William Meppem and Hannah Blackmore
Home Economists: Katja Harding-Irmer and Vikki-Leigh Moursellas
Recipe Transcriber: Sarah Williams
Photoshoot Co-ordinator/Head Cheerleader: Collette King
Production Director: Lou Playfair

ISBN 978 1 92235 152 4 Australia
ISBN 978 1 91166 835 0 UK

A catalogue record for this
book is available from the
National Library of Australia

A catalogue record for this book is available from
the British Library

Colour reproduction by Splitting Image Colour Studio Pty
Ltd, Clayton, Victoria
Printed by Hang Tai Printing Company Limited, China

OVEN GUIDE You may find cooking times vary depending on
the oven you are using. For fan-forced ovens, as a general rule,
set the oven temperature to 20°C (70°F) lower than indicated in the
recipe.

TABLESPOON MEASURES We have used 20 ml (4 teaspoon)
tablespoon measures. If you are using a 15 ml (3 teaspoon)
tablespoon add an extra teaspoon of the ingredient for
each tablespoon specified.

10 9 8 7 6 5 4 3 2 1